KU-021-842

LittleBrother

Published 2020.
Little Brother Books, Ground Floor, 23 Southernhay East, Exeter, Devon, EX1 1QL
Printed in Poland.
books@littlebrotherbooks.co.uk | www.littlebrotherbooks.co.uk

The Little Brother Books trademarks, logos, email and website addresses and the GamesWarrior logo and imprint are sole and exclusive properties of Little Brother Books Limited.

This is an unofficial and independently written book, the inclusion of any logos, images, quotes and references does

WHAT IS ROBLOX?

Roblox is a game creation platform like no other. If you just want to play games, you can find literally millions of titles to choose from. There's every kind of game you could ever want, from role-playing and job simulators to first person shooters and puzzles. Since players can easily upload their own games for the community, there's no shortage of fantastic titles and experience. They're all free too!

In addition, if you have an idea for a game and want to be more creative, Roblox Studio provides you the opportunity to make your own. Almost every game on the platform was created by players like yourself, so think about how cool it would be to have people interacting with something you created? Some creators even make a living actually designing and programming Roblox games!

Today Roblox is available on multiple platforms, and players have joined up by the millions to play all kinds of games.

There are over 100 million monthly active Roblox players, which means there are always plenty of people to team up with.

Some Roblox games have received over ONE BILLION visits!

CRAZY FACTS

Roblox was originally called DynaBlocks before being renamed.

David Baszucki and Erik Cassel created the beta version way back in 2004, but the full game didn't launch until 2006.

The official Roblox convention was first held in 2011. The annual Roblox Developers conference helps people learn about the latest features and how to make games.

Kids spend more time on Roblox than any site on the internet, and for teens it's second only to YouTube.

There are over 200 Roblox toys to collect, many of which offer exclusive codes for in-game content!

PLAYING ROBLOX EVERYWHERE

One of the best things about Roblox is that you can play it on almost any gaming platform!

Got a Windows or macOS desktop or laptop computer? You can play Roblox. Got an iOS or Android phone or tablet? You can play Roblox. Got an Xbox One and a 4K TV? You can play Roblox too. It's even available on Amazon Kindle tablets!

The best part is that no matter which platform you choose to log into, the game is the same and you will have access to your entire account. It doesn't matter where you are, you'll keep your progress in any games, friends lists and outfits.

NOW YOU'RE PLAYING WITH POWER

Of course, the desktop version of Roblox was the original, and also has access to the Roblox Studio. This handy option lets you make your very own games. You can't do that on a mobile app!

You can also use your computer's full power to enable Roblox in VR. Why play in Roblox when you can live in it? Roblox supports Oculus Rift and HTC Vive devices, allowing you to step foot into the 3D world and see what it really looks like to be a Robloxian. Many developers now design their games with VR in mind to make sure that you get the full Roblox experience!

DOUBLE YOUR FUN

Some players like to use the mobile version of Roblox as a chat app while playing on the desktop or console versions. This lets you hide the chat on the big screen and keep it from being too cluttered, and it also takes care of social features on your app.

what's up

stuff

want to play with me?

sure what

🐶 PET PARK🐶 Adopt Me

😺PET PARK UPDATE!🐱 ✨ Play with your pets and friends in the new park! 🚶

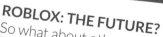
Play

ROBLOX: THE FUTURE?

So what about other games consoles? There's no word on Roblox appearing on other platforms just yet, but we'll have to wait and see. Roblox has constantly changed and evolved over the years!

XBOX ONE
ROBLOX BUNDLE

If you're new to the world of Roblox and want to dive straight in, then there's a great way to get started. You can pick up a fantastic Xbox One S bundle from Microsoft and Roblox that includes everything you need to get playing and creating!

XBOX ONE S

Included in the special £249.99 box is a white Xbox One S console that has a whopping 1TB hard drive. You'll definitely need all of that storage for software downloads, save games files and hi-res 4K screenshots of your creations.

FREE GAME DOWNLOAD

Once you've set up your snazzy new console, grab the Xbox Wireless controller included in the bundle and download your free-to-play copy of Roblox. You'll then be able to join millions of other gamers online around the world!

XBOX GAME PASS ULTIMATE

As well as Roblox, you can check out thousands of amazing titles for free with a one-month Xbox Game Pass. This is a great way to try out all kinds of games to see which ones you'd like to buy in full.

2,500 ROBUX

2,500 ROBUX
Level up your Roblox experience with some free cash. The Xbox One S bundle comes with a whopping 2,500 Robux, which you can use to buy new accessories and gear for your avatar or purchase add-on content for games.

EXCLUSIVE AVATARS
Also included with your new console are three exclusive avatars to download. Check out the clucking Brawk Tyson: Featherweight Champ, the mighty transforming Metal Menace Mech, or the Vengeful Samurai!

EXCLUSIVE ACCESSORIES
On top of everything else, you can download three exclusive accessories to use in the game. Kit out your Roblox avatar with the World Championship Belt, Mecha Domino Crown and Kidomaru the Cursed Blade!

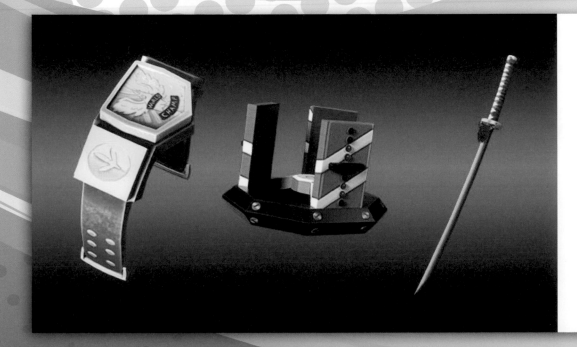

CUSTOMISING YOUR VERY OWN AVATAR

PERSONALISE

Avatar

The most important thing in Roblox is your in-game avatar. It represents you in the virtual world and you can change it to look however you like. You start with a basic appearance, but to be a true Robloxian you'll want to make your own character!

Characters **Body** Clothing Animation

Skin Hair Heads Faces Torsos

Characters Body **Clothing** Animation

Hats Shirts T-Shirts Pants Face

The Avatar section lets you change anything you like about your character. You can modify your model type to be sleek or blocky, tweak its height and weight and even the size of your head!

You're able to mix and match outfits for your avatar such as shirts, trousers and every kind of accessory you can imagine. You won't have much of a collection to start off with, but more items can be picked up in the Catalog.

ull Demon King

⬡ 250

Superhero

⬡ 230

Korblox Deathspeaker

⬡ 17,000

Magma Fiend
⬡ 300

Frost Guard General

Skeleton
⬡ 500

Are the thousands of options too overwhelming? Then simply select a pre-made character. They might not be as unique, but they still look cool.

| Characters | Body | Clothing | Animation | E |

Hats   Shirts   T-Shirts   Pants   Fac

You'll sometimes run into other players in Roblox wearing incredible outfits and not know where they got them from. Developers make their own unique characters for their games, so you'll often only be able to get the best outfits by playing your favourite games. Have a good look around!

GO MOBILE!

Avatar Editor

Explore the catalog to find more clothe

R6 **R15**

3D

| Recent | Clothing | Body | Animations |

Recent > All

Silly Fun   **Chill**   **City Life Woman -**   **City Life Woman -**

City Life Woman -   **City Life Woman -**   **City Life Woman - Left**   **City Life Woman - Face**

Body Type   100%

Scaling options are available under Body category. Check **Body > Scale**

Got it

Packages have been moved to Costumes. Check **Costumes > Preset Costumes**

Got it

Avatar isn't loading correctly?

Redraw

City Life Woman - Left   **Woman Right Arm**   **Woman Torso**   **Woman**

Woman Left Arm   **Woman Left Leg**   **Woman Face**   **Chestnut Bun**

Orange Beanie   **Knights of**   **Knights of**   **Knights of**

If you have Roblox on your mobile device, use the app to create avatars. Recent changes to the Avatar editor have made it easier to choose your look. You can save your favourite costumes and easily swap between them. You can also see immediately how your avatar looks and purchase items right at the bottom of the screen. It's much easier to customise your avatar using the app!

AVATARS IN YOUR HOME

Roblox teamed up with toy company Jazwares to create a massive collection of action figures, featuring some of the most popular in-game characters. Alongside the figures there are accessories, vehicles, game packs and even playsets to collect! Best of all, you get codes for virtual items when you buy Roblox toys, so you can dress up as them in your games too.

YOUR INVENTORY PAGE

As you play through Roblox, you'll end up collecting all sorts of items or buying them with hard-earned Robux. Fortunately, you can keep track of your various goodies by heading on over to your inventory page.

HOW TO VIEW YOUR INVENTORY

≡ ⬛ Games   Avatar Shop   Create   Robux   🔍 Search

- 🏠 Home
- 👤 Profile
- ✉️ Messages ①
- 👥 Friends
- 🧍 Avatar
- 📦 Inventory
- 🔄 Trade
- 👥 Groups
- 📰 My Feed
- 📑 Blog
- 🛒 Official Store
- 🎁 Gift Cards

Get Premium

Recommended   See All →

Your Bizarre Adventure [Story]	Creator Challenge Quiz	Piggy [ALPHA] VIP SERVER	Pizza Factory Tycoon	Hide and Seek Extreme	Kitty NEW ENDING!
👍 87% 👤 6.2K	👍 75% 👤 166	👍 91% 👤 119.4K	👍 88% 👤 4.3K	👍 91% 👤 13.7K	👍 86% 👤 26.5K

It's really easy to check out your inventory page online. Simply head to Roblox.com and click on the menu icon located at the top-left of the screen. This will open a dropdown menu and inventory is the sixth option.

INVENTORY CATEGORIES

Once you've selected inventory, you'll be able to see all of the items you've collected. These can be viewed in full or selected from the various categories listed on the left-hand side of the screen.

Category

- Accessories >
- Animations
- Audio
- Avatar Animations >
- Badges
- Decals
- Emotes
- Faces
- Game Passes
- Gear
- Heads
- Meshes
- Models
- Pants
- Places
- Plugins
- Shirts
- T-Shirts

Accessories › Hat

- Hat
- Hair
- Face
- Neck
- Shoulder
- Front
- Back
- Waist

Explore the catalog to find more Accessories! **Get More**

...nk Jelly ...orns By Erythia 120	FabergEgg of the New By ROBLOX Offsale	Egg of the High Skies By ROBLOX Offsale	Cooperative Cap By ROBLOX Offsale	Historic Headphones By ROBLOX Offsale
Doc Holidegg By ROBLOX Offsale	Shady Subjeggct By ROBLOX Offsale	Eggmunition By ROBLOX Offsale	Eg By ROBLOX Offsale	Eleggtrifying Eggmin of By ROBLOX Offsale	Star Creaeggtor By ROBLOX Offsale
Eggraging Shark of the By ROBLOX Offsale	Eggveloper Egg of "X,Y,Z" By ROBLOX Offsale	Tiny Tank Egg By ROBLOX Offsale	Robox By ROBLOX Free	Fintastic Headband By Simoon68 ◎ 80	Evil Side By maplestick ◎ 50

OTHER PLAYER'S INVENTORIES

As well as checking out your own haul, you can also take a look at what sort of goodies other players have collected! In addition to seeing what they have, you can also buy items from them with Robux.

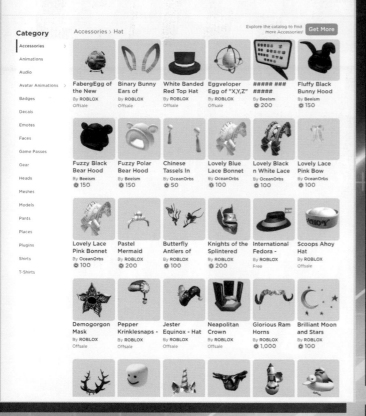

Category	Accessories > Hat				Explore the catalog to find more Accessories! **Get More**
Accessories					
Animations					
Audio					
Avatar Animations	FabergEgg of the New By ROBLOX Offsale	Binary Bunny Ears of By ROBLOX Offsale	White Banded Red Top Hat By ROBLOX Offsale	Eggveloper Egg of "X,Y,Z" By ROBLOX Offsale	##### ### ##### By Beeism ⊙ 200	Fluffy Black Bunny Hood By Beeism ⊙ 150
Badges					
Decals					
Emotes	Fuzzy Black Bear Hood By Beeism ⊙ 150	Fuzzy Polar Bear Hood By Beeism ⊙ 150	Chinese Tassels In By OceanOrbs ⊙ 50	Lovely Blue Lace Bonnet By OceanOrbs ⊙ 100	Lovely Black n White Lace By OceanOrbs ⊙ 100	Lovely Lace Pink Bow By OceanOrbs ⊙ 100
Faces					
Game Passes					
Gear	Lovely Lace Pink Bonnet By OceanOrbs ⊙ 100	Pastel Mermaid By ROBLOX ⊙ 200	Butterfly Antlers of By ROBLOX ⊙ 100	Knights of the Splintered By ROBLOX ⊙ 200	International Fedora - By ROBLOX Free	Scoops Ahoy Hat By ROBLOX Offsale
Heads					
Meshes					
Models	Demogorgon Mask By ROBLOX Offsale	Pepper Krinklesnaps - By ROBLOX Offsale	Jester Equinox - Hat By ROBLOX Offsale	Neapolitan Crown By ROBLOX Offsale	Glorious Ram Horns By ROBLOX ⊙ 1,000	Brilliant Moon and Stars By ROBLOX ⊙ 100
Pants					
Places					
Plugins					
Shirts					
T-Shirts					

SHOPPING TIME

Click on a player's item and you'll see what kind of accessory it is and how much it costs. Before you splash your cash, you can also try the item on your Roblox avatar and even check out how it looks in 3D!

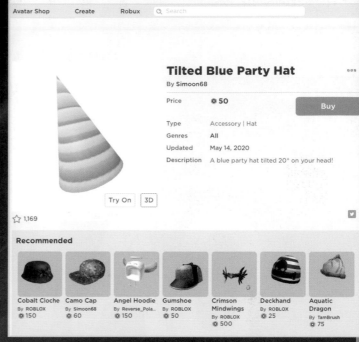

Avatar Shop   Create   Robux   Search

Tilted Blue Party Hat
By Simoon68

Price	⊙ 50	**Buy**
Type	Accessory	Hat	
Genres	All	
Updated	May 14, 2020	
Description	A blue party hat tilted 20° on your head!	

Try On   3D

⭐ 1,169

Recommended

Cobalt Cloche By ROBLOX ⊙ 150	Camo Cap By Simoon68 ⊙ 60	Angel Hoodie By Reverse_Pola... ⊙ 150	Gumshoe By ROBLOX ⊙ 50	Crimson Mindwings By ROBLOX ⊙ 500	Deckhand By ROBLOX ⊙ 25	Aquatic Dragon By TamBrush ⊙ 75

FREE ACCESSORIES

You don't always need to spend Robux on inventory items, as there's loads of free stuff to get. Just head to the Catalog (see p14-15), select 'Bestselling' and 'This Week' and grab everything you want!

Catalog

Category
View All Items
Featured
  All Featured Items
  Featured Accessories
  Featured Animations
  Featured Faces
  Featured Gear
  Featured Bundles
  Featured Emotes
Community Creations +
Collectibles +
Clothing +
Body Parts +
Gear
Accessories
Avatar Animations +

Filters
Genre
All Genres
☐ Building
☐ Horror
☐ Town and City
☐ Military
☐ Comedy
☐ Medieval
☐ Adventure
☐ Sci-Fi
☐ Naval
☐ FPS
☐ RPG
☐ Sports
☐ Fighting
☐ Western

Price
⦿ Any Price

Featured

True Blue Hair Free	Silly Fun Free	Chill Free
Lavender Updo Free	Orange Beanie with Black Hair Free	Happy New Year Rat Free
Jade Necklace with Shell Free	Salute Free	Medieval Hood of Mystery Free
Red Roblox Cap	Orange Shades	Roblox Visor

LEVELS AND MORE

As well as accessories and items to buy, players also show off other things in their inventories such as models and levels they've created. This is a great way to check out how creative players can be in the game.

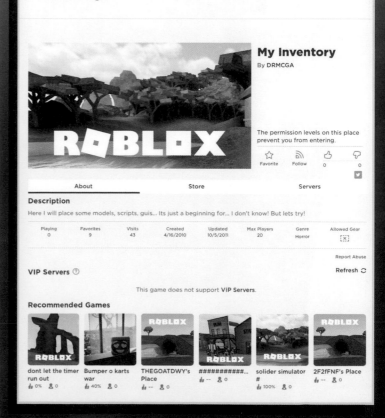

My Inventory
By DRMCGA

The permission levels on this place prevent you from entering.

Favorite   Follow   👍 0   👎 0

About   Store   Servers

Description
Here I will place some models, scripts, guis... Its just a beginning for... I don't know! But lets try!

Playing	Favorites	Visits	Created	Updated	Max Players	Genre	Allowed Gear
0	9	43	4/16/2010	10/5/2011	20	Horror	[×]

Report Abuse

VIP Servers ⓘ   Refresh ↻

This game does not support VIP Servers.

Recommended Games

dont let the timer run out 👍 0% 👤 0	Bumper o karts war 👍 40% 👤 0	THEGOATDWY's Place 👍 -- 👤 0	###########... # 👍 -- 👤 0	solider simulator 👍 100% 👤 0	2F2fFNF's Place 👍 -- 👤 0

Roblox is completely free, but you'll need to do some shopping if you want to buy new items for your avatar. The Roblox Catalog can be overwhelming at first – there's so much to look at!

BROWSING THE CATALOG

SHOP 'TIL YOU DROP

Featured › Featured Accessories

Relevance

International Fedora - Free	**Bear Face Mask** ◎ 100	**Platinum Bangs w bun** By Erythia ◎ 150	**Beautiful Hair for Beautiful** ◎ 95	**Galactic Wings** By supernob123 ◎ 600	**Classic Swordpack** ◎ 150
Blonde Cheerleading By Sukimeki ◎ 130	**White Luxury Backpack** By Myzta ◎ 150	**Fuzzy Polar Bear Hood** By Beeism ◎ 150	**Midnight Motor** ◎ 500	**Nariwear Futurist X** By intervin ◎ 150	**Holiday Crown** ◎ 50
Vintage Glasses By WhoToTrus ◎ 125	**Nephalem Wings** By Jazzyx3 ◎ 450	**Sparkling Angel Wings** ◎ 1,000	**Cinnamon Hair** ◎ 80	**Cyber Katanas** By supernob123 ◎ 200	**Demon Tail** By supernob123 ◎ 50

As well as official Roblox merchandise, there's lots of user-created content to grab and you'll never be without new things to try on. Sort items any number of ways to find the specific articles you need, from funky shorts to a cool backpack.

FIND WHAT YOU NEED

Filters

Genre

All Genres

- [ ] Building
- [x] Horror
- [ ] Town and City
- [ ] Military
- [ ] Comedy
- [ ] Medieval
- [ ] Adventure
- [ ] Sci-Fi
- [ ] Naval
- [ ] FPS
- [ ] RPG
- [ ] Sports
- [ ] Fighting
- [ ] Western

Price

◎ Any Price

Cookie ◎ 150
◎ 130

Mr. Whiskers ◎ 250

Bluesteel Claw ◎ 300

8-Bit Pumpkin   **Giant Ape**

Filter the Catalog by genre to find the best items to equip your character, if you want unique outfits for every type of game. Sort by 'Medieval' for an RPG, or 'Sports' for an Obby course. Playing a spooky game? Click on 'Horror' to throw an outfit together that even Dracula would appreciate.

FEATURED ITEMS

Featured Items on Roblox

| Bull Demon King ◎ 250 | Ninja Animation Package ◎ 750 | Bear Face Mask ◎ 100 | Superhero ◎ 230 | Cartoony Animation ◎ 250 |

| Korblox Deathspeaker ◎ 17,000 | Platinum Bangs w bun By Erythia ◎ 150 | Beautiful Hair for Beautiful ◎ 95 | Levitation Animation ◎ 1,000 | Magma Fiend ◎ 300 | Err... ◎ 70 |

| Stylish Animation | Robot Animation | Frost Guard General | Skeleton ◎ 500 | White Luxury Backpack | Galactic Wings |

The Featured Items tend to show the latest options. They're mostly official Roblox items, although they do feature ones from creators too. You can see who made each item, as well as how many people added it to their Favourites. Those tend to be the most popular, but also the most well-made!

KER-CHING!

Bull Demon King
By ROBLOX

Price	◎ 250		Buy
Type	Bundle		
Description	Bull Demon King is a brave warrior of the Tribe. Underneath his fierce appearance, he secretly longs for peace. His favorite hobby is taking care of cute critters.		

☆ 1,487   3D

Recommended

| Elemental Crystal Golem By ROBLOX ◎ 400 | Nick Bass By ROBLOX ◎ 250 | Davy Bazooka By ROBLOX ◎ 250 | Korblox Hunter By ROBLOX ◎ 1,000 | Blocky Mech By ROBLOX ◎ 450 | Barb the Barbarian By ROBLOX ◎ 800 | Mr. Toilet By ROBLOX ◎ 350 |

Included Items

One thing you'll notice is that nearly every item costs Robux! This is real-life money, so you might not have any to spend. Don't feel pressured into buying anything you don't want to. Remember, these outfits don't change anything about the game besides your the look of your avatar.

FREE STUFF

Featured › Featured Bundles

Price (Low to High) ▾
- Relevance
- Most Favorited
- Bestselling
- Recently Updated
- Price (High to Low)
- Price (Low to High)

| Oliver Free | ROBLOX Girl Free | Knights of Redcliff: Free | Woman Free | City Wor... Free |

| The High Seas: Beatrix The Free | Rthro Animation Free | Squad Ghouls: Drop Dead Free | Man Free | ROBLOX Boy Free | Summer Free |

| Robloxian 2.0 ◎ 15 | CoolKid McAwesome ◎ 30 | Action Figure ◎ 30 | The Finnster ◎ 50 | Snow Shredder ◎ 50 | Gunslinger ◎ 60 |

If you're tired of the standard boring items you're given when you create a Roblox account, fear not! There are a lot of free things you can buy and equip on your avatar. Use the drop-down menu on the top right of the Catalog to sort items by price, and easily find free stuff. Just click on the 'Get' button and it'll be added to your inventory. Head to the Avatar editor and you can put the item on.

SELL YOUR OWN

- Games
- Places
- Models
- Decals
- Badges
- Game Passes
- Audio
- Animations
- Meshes
- User Ads
- Sponsored Games
- Shirts
- T-Shirts
- Pants
- Plugins
- Developer Resources
  - Studio
  - Docs
  - Community

Translator Portal

Create a T-Shirt Don't know how? Click here

Find your image: Choose File No file chosen

T-Shirt Name: _____

Upload

T-Shirts

You haven't created any t-shirts.

Having trouble finding something you want to wear? Why not make your own? That's right, Roblox doesn't just let you make your own games, you can make your own outfits for your characters too. You can easily upload designs to the Roblox website and have your creations appear in the game, or choose to sell them in the Catalog for Robux!

Buy Robux

ROBUX
CURRENCY GUIDE

If you want premium items in Roblox, they're going to cost real-world cash. Roblox uses Robux as its currency for the entire platform. Every paid item in the Catalog uses Robux, as well as user-created items in games, such as game passes and clothing options. There are thousands of things you can buy with your Robux, so if there's a game you love, and you want to support its developer, the best way is to buy items from their game.

BUY CO?
Use coins to customize your meep, and more on MeepCit

| 400 coins | Most Popular! | 100 coin |
| BUY FOR 80 ROBUX | | R$ 200 |

| 2500 coins | 4600 coins 15% MORE! | 960 coi 20% |
| R$ 500 | R$ 800 | R$ 160 |

GIFT COINS

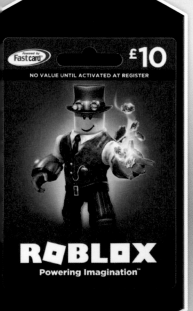

You can buy Robux through the game or website, or even pick up physical Robux gift cards in stores.

£4.59	⬡ 400
£8.99	⬡ 800
£18.49	⬡ 1,700
Value Packs	
£46.49	⬡ 4,500
£92.99	⬡ 10,000

Developers get paid in Robux, but they can cash out for real-world money. The current exchange rate is £0.0026 per Robux, or £265 USD for 100,000 Robux. That's a lot of T-shirt sales!

Element
By ROBLOX

Price	⬡ 4C
Type	Bundl
Description	The li summ glowi

Buy Robux

Get Robux to purchase upgrades for your avatar or buy special abilities in games. For more information on how to earn Robux, visit our **Robux Help page**. Purchase Roblox Premium to get more Robux for the same price. Roblox Premium is billed every month until cancelled. **Learn more here.**

	Buy Robux	Subscribe and get more!
£4.59	◎ 400	◎ 450/month
£8.99	◎ 800	◎ 1,000/month
£18.49	◎ 1,700	◎ 2,200/month

sufficient Robux

t have enough Robux to buy this

Current balance: ◎ 0

ancel   Buy Robux

Younger gamers should ask a parent before buying Robux. Roblox is mostly free to play, but Robux cost real money. Be sure you're allowed to buy some before your parents get a massive bill!

Get Item

Would you like to get the Hat "Roblox Baseball Cap" from ROBLOX for **Free**?

Get Now   Cancel

Your balance after this transaction will be ◎ 0

Never click on any links that say 'Free Robux', or any links from people you don't know. These could be scams or people trying to hack into your account. It's best to report anyone trying to offer you free Robux straight away!

A good rule of thumb is, if it sounds too good to be true, it probably is. No one is giving away money for free in Roblox!

DID YOU KNOW?

One Robux is actually called a 'Robuk'?

Robux used to be styled as R$ before switching to the gold symbol it is today.

Roblox used to have another currency called Tix, but it was abandoned.

◎ 400

◎ 800

◎ 1,700

trolled by
ke a giant

WHAT IS ROBLOX PREMIUM?

ROBLOX
PREMIUM

WHAT IT IS:

If you just can't get enough of Roblox, maybe it's time to join the club. Roblox Premium is a paid membership club that's only for the most devoted Robloxians, the ones that are already spending all their time and money in the game.

WHAT YOU GET:

You get a monthly allowance depending on how much you spend. Every month, you'll be given a set amount of Robux to spend, a special profile icon to show off that you're a member, and even more extra features.

Buy Robux

Get Robux to purchase upgrades for your avatar or buy special abilities in game. For more information on how to earn Robux, visit our **Robux Help page**. Purchase Roblox Premium to get more Robux for the same price. Roblox Pre... billed every month until cancelled. **Learn more here.**

	Buy Robux	Subscribe and get more!
£4.59	400	450/month
£8.99	800	1,000/month
£18.49	1,700	2,200/month

Creating the Trade

TRADE!
You can only trade between other Premium users, and not every item is available for trade, but it's a nice perk.

SELL!
Only Premium users can sell T-shirts, shirts and trousers. They earn 70% of the Robux, with 30% going to Roblox, so it's important to make your prices reasonable.

WHO SHOULD GET IT:
If you're developing Roblox games or looking to make money crafting items, you should definitely look into getting Roblox Premium.

Buy Robux™

Get Robux to purchase upgrades for your avatar or to buy special abilities in games.

Starter Kit	
R$ 440	£4.59
R$ 880	£8.99
R$ 1,870	£18.49
Super Value	
R$ 4,950	£46.49
R$ 11,000	£92.99

If you're already spending money on Robux you can save a bit with a membership, as long as you don't forget to spend all of your Robux every month.

WHO SHOULDN'T GET IT
Anyone who just wants to play games. This membership doesn't change anything about the game, and doesn't make it any more fun!

DID YOU KNOW?
Roblox Premium actually used to be called Builders Club, or BC, before it was renamed.

Outrageous Builders Club

With this Membership:

100 Active Places

A UNIVERSE OF GAMES

Roblox allows players to create literally any kind of game they can think of. Plus, so many Roblox games are unlike anything else out there, combining multiple genres for unique experiences. This may be why Roblox has removed the ability to sort games by type, but still, many of its biggest games fit into specific genres. Here are some of the most popular kinds to play!

TOWN AND CITY
These are games set inside cities or towns, with more modern settings than most titles. Things can still get weird, but the locations will always look familiar.

ADVENTURE

It's time to set forth on an epic adventure! In these games you embark on quests as the hero, exploring locations and seeking to save the world.

HORROR

Only for the very bravest of Robloxians! These are scary games, meant to make you jump in your seat. You might see some spooky things here - that are definitely NOT for very young gamers. You have been warned!

RPG

Role Playing Games are always fun – who doesn't want to try to play as someone else? If you love fantasy games, here's the genre for you, as there are plenty of swords and sorcery for true RPG fans.

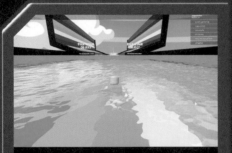

OBBY

These are Roblox versions of obstacle courses. They're super fun and tricky. Try to get to the end of the courses without getting knocked out!

SPORTS

Recreations of popular sports titles, as well as brand new sports made just for Robloxians!

FPS

First person shooters, like Call of Duty, made with Roblox. You have to blast other players while avoiding their attacks!

BEWARE OF FAKES!

Make sure that the game you're looking for is the real one. Lots of sneaky people try to name their creations almost exactly the same as popular titles in order to fool players into checking out their titles instead. They're almost never as good, so don't fall for it!

ADOPT ME

Creator: DreamCraft (NewFissy, Bethink)
Release Date: July 2017
Genre: RPG

Ever want to make your very own family, but without all of the responsibility? Adopt Me allows you to do just that! Get ready to explore the world with your new family and improve your home too.

You'll first pick one of two teams – Baby or Parent. Both will spawn inside their homes, but to start with you'll be alone. Now it's time to make your own family! Simply go up to nearby players and ask to be part of their family.

1

If you're playing as a baby, you don't need a parent! Just take care of yourself. Parents earn points by taking care of their baby's needs, so it makes sense for them to work together. The four basic needs are:

2

HUNGER – how hungry the baby is. Pick up lots of formula and food to make sure your baby doesn't starve.

FUN – how active the baby is. Bring your child to the park and shake a rattle at it to give it a more exciting day. You can even take your whole family out for activities, like balloon rides and bungee jumping!

CLEANLINESS – how clean the baby is. Make sure to give your baby showers (or just take it for a swim at the pool in town) to wipe off all of that yucky drool and baby grime.

SLEEPINESS – how tired the baby is. Your baby needs plenty of rest in their crib!

If you have even more love to give, you can also adopt pets – everything from dogs and cats to unicorns! They have the same basic needs as babies, but they look a lot cooler.

HOME SWEET HOME
The best part about Adopt Me is making your own unique house. It starts off empty, but you can transform it however you like, as long as you have enough money.

BUCK GUIDE

Here are some tips on getting lots of money to upgrade your look and the appearence of your house:

- Play the game every day and you'll get a login bonus. Keep the streak going fo five days for a Mystery Gift!
- Playing as a Baby? Get a pet and you can double your chances for money.
- The Lemonade Stand offers Lemonade for a dollar – the cheapest drink in the game. Or you can steal an apple from your teacher at school!
- Hang out at the playground to eliminate boredom. It's free and always fun.
- Money Trees can be bought for $1450 bucks. It's steep, but if you play a lot they'll eventually pay for themselves. Note: you can only collect $100 a day.

One of the most popular games in Roblox, MeepCity allows you to become part of a virtual world. Up to 100 players can play together, exploring the world, partying, enjoying some fishing, or even kart racing!

Creator: Alexnewtron
Release Date: February 2016
Genre: Town and City

meepcity

MeepCity gives you a home in the Neighbourhood, which looks pretty small and empty to start with. It's a tiny one-bedroom home with no furniture, but within minutes you can outfit it with all kinds of accessories. To earn new stuff, you'll need coins, the currency of the game.

Getting That Coin

You can earn coins just by playing the game. They'll roll into your bank account as you walk around and hang out. If you want more, you'll need to work for it. Head to the Playground and beyond and you'll see a ton of stuff to do in the city. The shops are here and a few opportunities to earn coins. Little minigames such as shoveling snow, to thrilling ones like kart racing all give you cash!

Fish For Cash

Upgrade your fishing rod ASAP. Rare fish give you plenty of coins.

Play nice. Friends can send each other gifts, including furniture, even if the player is offline!

It's Party Time

The Party tent is where you go to chill. Buy a MeepCity Plus pass and you can even host your own party!

Instant Travel

Overwhelmed by everything going on in the city? Don't forget that if you click on your profile you can just teleport to your favourite places

Go MeepCity Racing

This will seem familiar to any fans of plumber-based racing games. Do your best to drift to first place, using any of the power ups you come across. Higher places get more coins, so aim for first!

Play Star Ball

Roll your ball to the end point, trying to pick up stars along the way. This Obby game is tons of fun. Try your best to get all three stars each level, to get the most coins!

DID YOU KNOW?

You can get a pet Meep and buy all kinds of fun accessories for it!

Despite only being released a few years ago, MeepCity was the first game to hit a billion visits!

There are tons of stores to check out in the Plaza, like a Pizza Place, Ice Cream Parlour, and even a handy hospital.

It's time to play cops and robbers!

This is a team-based game and there are three you can play as – Prisoners, Police, and Criminals. You can only choose Prisoners or Police when you start though, as Criminals are escaped Prisoners (who get up to all sorts of mischief and mayhem).

Creator: Badimo
Release Date: January 2017
Genre: Town and City

JAILBREAK

PRISONERS

You escaped!
You are now a criminal. Run, hide, rob banks, check out the city, find other criminals. Don't get caught!

Prisoners don't want to be stuck in Prison. Fortunately this place has really terrible security and there are all kinds of ways to escape. You can steal an officer's keycard, blow up a wall, or even crawl out through the sewers. If an officer catches you, you'll be thrown back into your cell, so you'll have to be sneaky.

You won't have weapons unless you break into the Security office somehow, or pickpocket a police officer, so for the most part you'll be defenceless. Officers have guns and can taze or handcuff you if you're not careful. Use your wits and try to appear as if you're a model prisoner!

POLICE

If you're playing as the Police, your job is to keep prisoners inside and to apprehend any that escape. Fortunately you spawn with a bunch of items in your inventory that can help you – a pistol, handcuffs, taser and spike trap.

You can shoot or arrest prisoners if they're up to no good, or if they're caught trespassing in an area they're not supposed to be in. However, you can't just overstep the rules of the job! If you shoot or apprehend someone who is innocent, you will lose valuable money that you'll need for new weapons and vehicles.

Officers can jump in ultra-fast cop cars to catch Criminals who are causing chaos in the nearby city. Alarms will ring when Criminals are on the prowl and you'll earn money for taking them down. Buy new weapons and vehicles with the cash you earn to help your quest!

CRIMINALS

Criminals can plan robberies and heists to get money to buy new goodies. This includes everything from weapons and vehicles to apartments. Once you start committing crimes, such as robbing a petrol station, bank, or museum, you will earn a bounty. The higher your bounty, the more the Police will want to arrest you and claim your bounty – so beware! Criminals with the highest bounties will make it on to the 'Top Criminals' board in the prison, so their performance can be tracked.

Criminals are faster than Police, but they're not faster than bullets. They are, however, able to get more money than any other team. It's a dangerous life, but it pays while it lasts!

WORK AT A PIZZA PLACE

Creator: Dued1
Release Date: March 2008
Genre: Job Simulator

Wait – why would you want to go to work in your own video game? Turns out that getting a job at this pizza place is way more fun than working at a real one! Up to 12 players can join forces to earn coins and bring joy to the people of their local town. You live here too and if you earn enough money you can customise and decorate your home, and even order your own pizza!

The best part about this game are the different roles you can try out. Here are the jobs on the menu:

CASHIER:

Wait for customers to walk up to the counter or drive up and take their order. Sometimes real players will even show up! As cashier you'll have to ask the customer what they want and pick from the correct items on the register, which will send an order to the back of the restaurant. Pick the wrong item and the customer will complain and leave without ordering.

You need to be on point here, because people will leave if you are rude to them, or if they have to wait too long for their order.

COOK:

After the cashier enters the order, it will appear on the board in the kitchen. Your job is to then cook the pizzas! You'll have to grab the correct ingredients and add them to the dough before cooking it in the oven. You'll need to make sure not to overcook the pizza or it could burn and start a fire, making people scramble for a fire extinguisher!

After you have a perfectly cooked pizza, you then need to send it to be boxed for delivery.

PIZZA BOXER:

Pick this role and your job is to grab the pizzas as they appear and place them in an open boxes. Close the box and you can send it to a conveyer belt that shuttles it along to the next role. This is probably the easiest job in the whole game!

DELIVERY:

In this job you'll be getting pizzas to customers as fast as possible. Once you grab a box, it will tell you which address to take it to. Get a car from outside and drive it to the house's mailbox. Make sure you get the right address though, or you'll really annoy someone.

SUPPLIER:

The supplier has to load a truck with supplies. You'll see which boxes are required, and it's your job to pick the correct ones. Drive them to the pizzeria's conveyer belt, where you'll then load all of the boxes.

MANAGER:

This is the boss! They have to hand out pay, fire (votekick) terrible workers, and even name players 'Employee of the Day'. Just like in real-life, Managers sometimes have to step into other roles in order to help out. There's only one manager at a time, although people can vote to remove them if they're not doing their job properly.

MONEY:

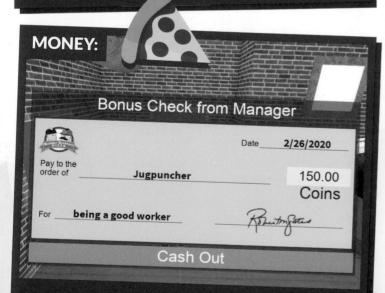

Bonus Check from Manager

Date: 2/26/2020

Pay to the order of: Jugpuncher

150.00 Coins

For: being a good worker

Cash Out

You earn Money (Coins) through being paid, and can use cash to buy extras for your home! The bigger the house upgrade, the more furniture and decorations you can add. Find a good pizza crew and you'll earn enough in no time!

DID YOU KNOW?

Work at a Pizza Place was one of the first games released on Roblox!

It has received over TWO BILLION visits.

You can eventually upgrade your house into a massive mansion!

There's a secret room near the drive-thru (look for the darker bricks)!

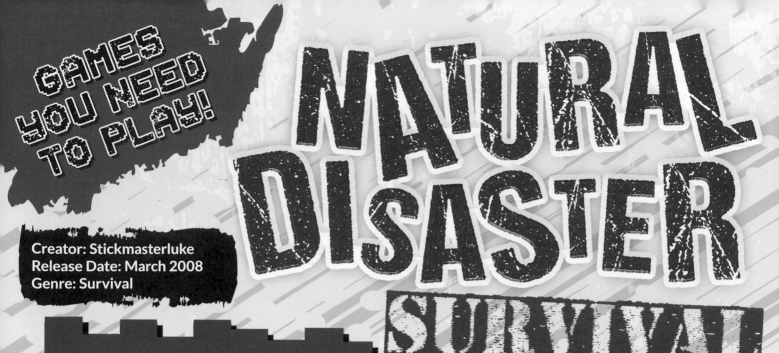

NATURAL DISASTER SURVIVAL

Creator: Stickmasterluke
Release Date: March 2008
Genre: Survival

You're stuck on a deserted island with other players, and only have seconds before extreme weather hits. You'll face round after round of catastrophes, and never have any idea what's coming next!

There are 11 different disasters that can take place over 18 different maps. You only have a few seconds after starting a round to figure out what you should do. Buying milk and bread won't help you here – you'll have to think quickly to stay alive. Your health will carry over between rounds, so avoiding any damage is key.

If you're not sure how to survive a particular disaster, a good idea is to follow other players and see where they go. If a lot of people are heading to a particular location, they've probably survived this kind of disaster before.

Unlike other Roblox games, Natural Disaster Survival has fall damage! It may seem like a good idea to climb a tower to avoid a tsunami, but if it knocks you off, you won't make it.

THE MAPS

1. TRAILER PARK
2. ARCH PARK
3. RAVING RACEWAY
4. RAKISH REFINERY
5. FURIOUS STATION
6. LAUNCH LAND
7. SAFETY SECOND
8. PRISON PANIC
9. HAPPY HOME
10. SKY TOWER
11. FORT INDESTRUCTIBLE
12. GLASS OFFICE
13. SURF CENTRAL
14. COASTAL QUICKSTOP
15. HEIGHTS SCHOOL
16. LUCKY MART
17. PARTY PALACE
18. SUNNY RANCH

THE DISASTERS

1. FLASH FLOOD: A dark cloud will appear in the sky before the island starts to flood with water. Make sure to keep to high ground.

2. METEOR SHOWER: Rocks rain down from the sky, destroying anything they touch. It will destroy bricks too, so keep an eye on the sky and run when you see one coming.

3. BLIZZARD: A dark cloud brings snow, which will freeze anyone stuck outside. Head indoors ASAP!

Disaster Warning:
Blizzard! Seek warmth and find shelter

4. SANDSTORM: Very similar to Blizzard, but blocks get thrown around too. Avoid them because they really, really hurt!

5. ACID RAIN: A dark cloud appears in the sky before it starts to rain acid that will damage players. Stay inside and watch out for puddles of acid!

6. EARTHQUAKE: The ground will start to shake and throw everything around, including you! Stay away from the ocean and beware of falling structures!

7. VOLCANIC ERUPTION: A volcano erupts right next to the ocean and starts shooting out lava. Stay far away from it, avoid all of the lava blocks and dodge any incoming projectiles to survive!

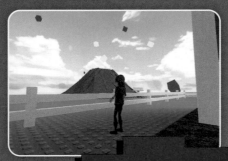

8. TORNADO: A tornado appears in the center of the map and starts swirling throughout, destroying everything it touches. Stay as far away from it as you can get!

9. TSUNAMI: You'll see a massive wave appear far from the island and start moving towards the island. Head to the top of a structure but make sure it's not a weak one, as it will damage everything in its path.

10. FIRE: A section of the map will ignite, starting a fire that spreads along any bricks near it. Try and stay away from anything flammable at all costs!

11. THUNDERSTORM: Lightning will begin to strike the map in different areas. Try and stay indoors because they will zap you with one shot!

DID YOU KNOW?

If you have Robux, use the green balloon! It's a really handy way to avoid disaster.

The only way to heal yourself is with the apple, so consider it if your health is low.

Taking the high ground is usually a good idea, but not so much if an earthquake destroys your structure.

Developer Stickmasterluke's game was the first to receive 10 million visits!

SUPER HERO TYCOON

BANG!

While this great tycoon game allows you to start a superhero business, the best part is it also allows you to roleplay as your favourite superheroes!

Creator: Super Heroes™
Release Date: December 2016
Genre: Tycoon

ZAP!

When you first spawn in the game you'll see that you're surrounded by various superhero franchises. Other players may have claimed some of these, but some are empty and waiting for a new owner! Just look at the signs in front of each property that reveal which hero lives there, choose the one you like best, and claim the plot.

Now it's time for you to become a superhero and get all their unique gadgets! But before you can start playing with all of these items, the first thing you'll need is money.

Your cash will build up over time and you can collect it from a console near the front door. Once you have a steady stream of money coming in, you can use your cash to upgrade various parts of the building. Some of the upgrades will increase the amount of revenue coming in, so go for those first to make things faster.

PoW

Once you have enough money you can purchase display cases that contain unique gadgets and weapons for your superhero of choice! You'll earn some amazing powers and be able to test them out on all of your neighbouring heroes. Random boxes drop outside containing weapons, as well as cash.

It's usually a free-for-all outside, but fortunately you can hide out in your fortress of solitude. With your money you can build defences for your home. Start with basic things like walls and ceilings, as well as a laser grid for your front door that will zap annoying trespassers.

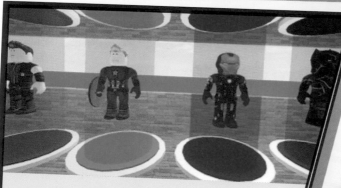

Keep building and you'll get access to a second floor, where you can unlock your costumes. One of the best things about this game are the kinds of heroes on offer. They're rotated often, but you can often catch real (user-created) superheroes here. Good luck in your epic battles!

DID YOU KNOW?

You can purchase handy upgrades which double your cash rate with handy Robux.

When an upgrade is green, you have enough money to then buy it.

Red means you'll need to wait.

Other players can grab your hero's gadgets, but they can't touch your cash.

ROYALE High

Creator: callmehbob
Release Date: April 2017
Genre: Adventure

This magical school has attracted a massive audience, as the game allows you to customise your character in all sorts of great ways. You can go to classes and do homework while showing off your outfits. You'll receive Diamonds (the game's currency) every time you level up, so it pays to be a good student. Use Diamonds to unlock new accessories and outfits. Do well enough and you'll transform into a princess or prince!

SCHOOL TIPS

Do your homework on time! Beat the deadline to make sure you achieve a good grade in each class. The higher your grade, the more your student star will fill up. Once it's full you'll get lots of Diamonds!

Bring your books to class for extra XP. Drop them off at your locker and grab new ones between classes. Remember that everyone at this fairy school can fly – double jump and you'll take to the sky.

CLASSES

ART

You're given a painting to look at and a canvas to recreate it. If you manage to paint it faster than any of your classmates, you'll get an A+. You can still get an A, as long as you finish it correctly.

BAKING

Just like in real-life, baking is all about following recipes. Choose a baking station and do a number of tasks in order to ensure you make something tasty. You'll be graded depending on how much you can finish in time!

CHEMISTRY

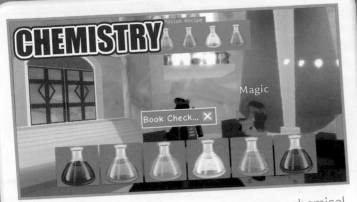

Listen to the instructions and perform some chemical reactions. Each round is different and only the players who have won at least one round will get an A.

CODING

This is more of a typing class than coding. You will see letters appear on the screen and have to type them quickly and correctly. A+ students are faster than any other, but this class is an easy A.

ENGLISH

The teacher will put up a sentence on the whiteboard and you have to click the one that doesn't have any errors.

PE

There are all kinds of obstacles to beat, such as a pool, race track and trampolines. Get to the end first to earn an A grade!

SWIMMING

Swimming is probably pretty hard with wings, but you can do it! Jump over the pole as it comes near you and try not to fall.

WORK HARD, PLAY HARD

Go to school, do well, and you'll be able to relax in a number of ways. Shopping is a big part of the game, and the more Diamonds you earn the more intricate costumes you'll be able to afford!

DID YOU KNOW?

Players whose designs are chosen to be in the game receive a special badge!

Developer Callmebob wants to make Royale University next.

There are two Royale High toys you can buy that give you exclusive items and 2000 Diamonds!

Make sure to stick to the beauty pageant's theme on Sunset Island to win big.

BEE SWARM SIMULATOR

Creator: Onett
Release Date: March 2018
Genre: Adventure

If the thought of beekeeping gives you a bit of a buzz, here's the perfect game for you!

Bee Swarm Simulator allows you to raise your very own hive of bees, exploring a world full of flowers and strange creatures.

BEE-GINNING THE GAME

The first thing you have to do each time you start up the game is to claim one of the many hives near the spawn point.

Put eggs into the hexagonal holes in order to hatch different types of bees. This is where they'll live and head home to once they're tired.

BEE-COMING A GOOD NEIGHBOUR

There are lots of bears hanging around, all of which have a number of quests for you. If you do things for them they'll give you treats, which will upgrade your bees and hive! As you look around you'll find lots of flower patches, each of which is named after the items they're near. Go to them and start using your tool to collect pollen. Your swarm of bees will help out too!

Bee Bear
I'm Bee Bear! The magical mascot of Beesmas (within the context of Bee Swarm).

UPGRADING YOUR BEE-LONGINGS

You're only able to carry a tiny amount of pollen before having to go back to the hive and have your bees transform it into honey. You can upgrade your equipment so that you can carry much more pollen, as well as extract more with every swipe of your tool.

You can even eventually get items like parachutes to get to new areas and sprinklers that will allow flowers to grow back more quickly!

ALWAYS BEE QUESTING

The best way to progress in the game is to have lots of quests going all at once! Try to meet as many new bears as you can.

As you expand your hive you'll be able to access even more locations and more quests. Work on multiple quests at the same time and become a true bee expert!

Polar Bear

If you collect the ingredients, I'll cook us up something good.

DID YOU KNOW?

You can actually hatch Mythic bees that are super powerful, and super rare. See if you can find a 1 in 25,000 bee!

Some enemies only appear at night! Look for strange items sticking out of the ground...

There are all sorts of hidden items to be found. Make sure to explore every area of the world.

Creator: Coeptus
Release Date: November 2014
Genre: Simulation

WELCOME TO BLOXBURG

PAY TO PLAY

Unlike some Roblox games, Welcome To Bloxburg is a paid access title that will cost you 25 Robux to play. Once you've been given access, you'll enter a world with up to 12 players on one server.

If you want to play a Roblox game that's a bit more grounded in reality, then check out Welcome To Bloxburg. This life-simulation title is a huge hit that's had over 2 billion visits since its launch!

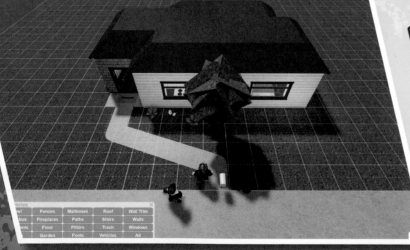

BUILD MODE

In the game, players can construct their own houses near a big city. Selecting 'Build Mode' allows you to initially make a one-story house on a 30x30 plot of land. Bigger properties require gamepasses to be bought before you can start adding to your house.

GAMEPASSES

To get even further into Welcome To Bloxburg you'll need to purchase gamepasses. These allow you to add extra floors and space to your house, double daily rewards, play cool tunes and even become an Excellent Employee!

JOBS

To pay for your new house you'll need to get some work! There are 12 jobs to choose from in the game, each of which pays a different amount. Complete tasks to get promoted and earn money to buy all sorts of stuff.

You received a paycheck!

1294

6/18/2020 DATE

PAY TO THE ORDER OF   mattdyuk $ 88.00

Eighty-Eight   DOLLARS

FOR   Working as Janitor   _Mr Blox_
000000379   000000824   1000

Cash Out

SKILLS TO PAY THE BILLS

By completing specific tasks, players will also be rewarded with additional skills. The eight skills currently in the game are: Athletic, Cooking, Gaming, Gardening, Intelligence, Music, Painting and Writing.

LOTS OF LOCATIONS

There are all sorts of locations to check out in the city. At some you'll be able to get a job, while others offer all sorts of items to buy for your avatar or house such as food, drinks, furniture and decorations.

BLOXBUSTER

Welcome To Bloxburg has been a massive success and been the favourite title of over 6.5 million players. That makes it one of the most successful Roblox games to date, even though it's pay to play.

FLEE THE FACILITY

Creator: A.W. Apps
Release Date: July 2017
Genre: Escape/Horror

Looking for a spooky game of hide and seek? See if you can flee the facility and escape the Beast!

This is a multiplayer game where one player plays as the Beast and has to hunt down up to four other players (or 'Survivors') and capture them in cryogenic pods before they escape. They will have to find and hack a number of computers in order to open the exit and get out alive!

islas0725pedro

PLAYING AS THE BEAST

Play as the Beast and you'll spawn into an enclosed room as the Survivors get a 15 second head start. Choose one of four abilities, although only 'Runner' is available when you start, which lets you run super-fast for a short time. You'll then spawn into the map and have to hunt down the survivors.

The Beast sees the world in a first-person perspective, which makes it a little harder to move around. The survivors are trying to find computers to hack to open the exits, so you've got to stop them. Fortunately, they're loud! You'll hear them clacking away at their keyboards and if they mess up the hacking mini-game, a red icon will appear giving away their exact position.

Your one weapon is a giant hammer that can be used to knock out your victims, who will crumple to the ground with one hit. If you click on an unconscious survivor, you'll tie them up and leash them to you. You then have to drag the helpless survivor to a cryogenic chamber somewhere on the map. Place a survivor in there and its health will start to dwindle before it finally freezes! Other survivors can rescue their friends and can also fall off the leash if you're not paying attention while you drag them.

YOU ARE THE BEAST
Hunt down and capture all of the survivors.
Hit survivors twice to drag them.
Drag survivors to freezing pods.

PICK A SPECIAL POWER

HACKER	RUNNER	SEER	STALKER
Not available	Gain a short boost of speed.	Not available	Not available
TBA		TBA	TBA

Capture all the survivors and you'll win, but be careful! If they manage to hack all of the computers, two exits will open up on the map and they will run for safety. Get them as fast as you can before they escape!

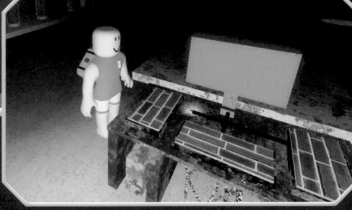

PLAYING AS THE SURVIVOR

Depending on how many players are in the game, your team will have to hack three to five computers to open the exit. You'll have a 15 second head start, so get cracking!

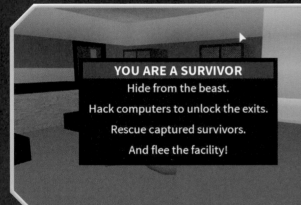

YOU ARE A SURVIVOR
Hide from the beast.
Hack computers to unlock the exits.
Rescue captured survivors.
And flee the facility!

The first thing you'll need to do is find the computers. Click on one and you'll begin hacking it, but be warned – it makes noise that the Beast can hear, and a little mini-game will pop up occasionally that requires a precise button press. If you mess that up, you'll stop hacking and an icon will reveal your exact location to the Beast!

If the Beast is close the music will change and you'll hear a heartbeat. You're a real target while hacking, so if you hear something you might want to look for somewhere to hide!

If the Beast gets you, he'll drag you to a cryogenic chamber to freeze, although your friends can save you. Sometimes the Beast will hang out near the chamber and try to grab your would-be rescuers.

Once all the computers have been hacked, you're almost free. The exits will appear on your map and the Beast's, too. It's not as simple as just opening a door, though – that would be too easy. Opening it makes loud noises and takes a little bit of time and the Beast will be looking to stop you no matter what. Good luck!

DID YOU KNOW?

There's a one-minute intermission between every game. During this time you can vote on the next map and spend currency in the Trade Hub for different cosmetics, such as new hammers.

Survivors can lay down, which allows them to hide under tables and crawl through vents. The Beast can't fit in these small holes so they're great for quick escapes!

The Beast is slower at jumping through windows and opening doors. Remember this when it's on your trail!

ARSENAL

Get ready to fight! If you're looking for some intense first-person action, here's your game. Join up with a crew to fight opposing teams using a massive amount of weapons!

Creator: ROLVe Community
Release Date: August 2015
Genre: First-person Shooter

Arsenal is based on Counter-Strike: Global Offensive (CS:GO)'s popular 'Gun Game' mode. In this first-person game you start with a random weapon and get a different one every time you eliminate an opponent. This makes for fast and frantic battles, as you run around a number of maps trying to get your foes before they get you.

Arsenal's greatest strength is its weapon list, which is fully loaded. This includes everything from shotguns and rifles to crossbows and rocket launchers – even pizza slices and snowballs!

While dozens of weapons keep you guessing at what's next, there are many ways to play the game, too.

THE GAME MODES OF ARSENAL

STANDARD
This is by far the most popular mode. Every time you take out another player your weapon will change, leaving you constantly figuring out how to fight. Sometimes you'll be given a super-powerful weapon like a rocket launcher, while other times you'll end up with a small pistol. You can't change weapons until you eliminate a player though. Once you rack up a number of kills you'll get the Golden Knife. Take someone out with this to win the match for your team!

GUN ROTATION

In this mode every person gets the same random gun, but it changes every 20 seconds. This means that no one will have an advantage over anyone else, although it also means that you need to really know how to fight with each and every weapon. If you get 30 kills you'll need to take out two people in order to get the Golden weapon and win the match!

CONCUSSION MANIA

Get ready for explosions! In this mode everyone only has one gun, the Concussion Rifle, and you need 16 kills to win. There's no Golden Weapon required. The Concussion Rifle is a bolt-action rifle that shoots rockets, with each round doing 50 damage to an enemy. You can also use it to rocket jump, meaning that this mode will see players flying all over the map!

RANDOMIZER

This is similar to Standard, in which weapons randomly change, but this time the weapon changes after you die. This means if you get a good one, you're going to want to stay alive as long as possible and take out as many of the opposing team as you can! Matches last four minutes and the team with the most points at the end wins.

COMPETITIVE

There's no Golden Knife in this mode, just the Golden Gun. There's also a much smaller batch of weapons available, and no projectile or explosive ones at all. Expect some truly hard matches here!

DID YOU KNOW?

Arsenal won three trophies at the Bloxy Awards – Best Sound Design, Best Game Trailer and Game of The Year.

You can rocket jump by pointing an explosive weapon at your feet and jumping as you fire. You'll take a little damage, but be able to propel yourself onto rooftops!

If you earn the 'Delivery' badge in Work at a Pizza Place you'll unlock a Pizza Boy skin in Arsenal.

Creator: Ready, Set, Play
Release Date: May 2019
Genre: MMORPG

ADVENTURE UP!

Looking for a fantasy world you can make your own? Adventure Up! allows players to delve into dungeons and fight monsters, or just explore the world and learn a new profession! There are lots of ways to play this game and the more you do the closer you'll be to becoming a super-powered, magic-wielding hero.

LOBBY

The Lobby is the town where you start. Here you'll find everything you need to prepare yourself for the next stage of your adventure. There are multiple shops to visit to buy, craft and upgrade your weapons and equipment. You'll see lots of people wandering around and you can chat with folks and get them to join your party on adventures.

There are also some fun activities to take part in, such as Training Dummies that allow you to test out your new weapons, Time Trials to attempt and even a Hot Air Balloon ride that lets you see the beautiful sights of the town from a bird's eye view.

EXPLORE

Wander around the world to level up, gather resources for crafting and gain lots of loot! Each map offers a different assortment of materials to collect, allowing you to level up by foraging, mining, or woodcutting. The Explore levels are where you can work on your professions, which is more exciting than it sounds.

You'll start off in Pleasant Valley and soon realize that there are enemies to fight (Blue Slimes! Orcs!) to earn experience points (XP), trees to chop down, ore to mine and plants to forage. Each map has unique materials to find, so you'll want to earn as much XP as you can in order to unlock new maps. Everything you do will level up one of your professions, so any time spent here will help you out when you get to the meat of the game, the Adventures!

Lobby

CHOP TREES

CRAFT GEAR / MAKE POTIONS

NE ORE

FORAGE

Sheathe weapons

Health   250 / 250

ADVENTURE

As you'd expect, these are the dungeons. Expect lots of intense combat when you step into one of these and make sure to join up with a good crew of heroes in town before setting out! Your team can mean all the difference between success and failure. As with Explore, the higher your level the more places you'll be able to access, from the dreary Crystal Caverns all the way up to the active volcano Mount Ashea

The first dungeon is Crystal Caverns, a smallish one that sees you fighting your way through crystal-infected miners before facing the massive Crystal Lord itself. You might have to make your way through it a few times before leveling up enough to access the next dungeon, but each time you can try out new skills you've learned and equipment you've found!

Crystal Caverns

PROFESSIONS

These are skills that you learn in the game. Each of them can be leveled up by simply performing the action. So if you want to get better at crafting, craft items. If you want to get better at mining, mine! It's important to get good at as many of these as possible.

MINING

Mining earns you ore, which you can use to craft into tools and weapons. The higher your level, the better the kind of ore you can mine, from Copper all the way up to Mystium. Mining is also crucial for clearing rubble in dungeons to find secret areas and loot!

WOODCUTTING

While exploring, cut down every tree you can find and you can use the logs you get for all sorts of items. It's important to level up this profession as you need it to find secret areas and loot behind wood planks in dungeons!

ALCHEMY

Used to craft potions. This is essential for later dungeons, as you'll be able to make health and regeneration potions, as well as others that increase your attack damage, speed and chances of getting good loot!

FORAGING

This is easy enough to do, as you just pick flowers and berries and roots that you come across while exploring.

CRAFTING

By crafting you'll be able to utilise all of the materials you find on your travels and turn them into new weapons, armour and accessories. Ore can be melted down into bars, which can be used for items of that material. The higher your level, the more things you can make!

FORAGING UP
8

Foraging   3s
Health   250 / 250

DID YOU KNOW?

There's a Daily Reward treasure chest available in the Lobby every day. Don't miss it!

Gems can provide tremendous upgrades for equipment, so slot them in when you find them.

You can select the difficulty of a dungeon, which then determines how hard the enemies are and how good the loot will be!

Bosses can appear in Explore levels, and give tons of XP. Keep an eye out for them!

Creator: RedManta Project 3
Release Date: January 2019
Genre: MMORPG

WORLD//ZERO

Get ready to enter an epic fantasy world packed with strange creatures, powerful magic and epic quests. This great Roblox game is well worth checking out if you like RPGs and challenging dungeon crawlers.

THE ADVENTURE BEGINS

Players first enter a massive open world setting and have to choose from one of three starter class characters. These are the Swordmaster, Mage and Defender and each has their own unique abilities.

LEVEL UP

By completing quests and defeating enemies, your character will begin to level up. This allows you to unlock powerful subclasses at Level 15 and Level 30, giving you access to even more amazing abilities.

JOIN FORCES

You'll definitely need to have strength in numbers to take on all of the challenges in World//Zero. Up to 12 players can come together in one game and help each other out, making survival more likely.

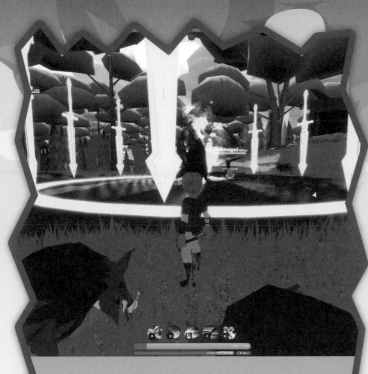

COLLECT PETS

You can get even more help in the game by collecting and evolving your very own pets. These handy animals include cats, rats, foxes, wolves and more, all of which will fight alongside you in battles.

Monsters drop Pet Food!

I always remember to feed my pet berries!

TOUGH BOSSES

One great way to level up is to join forces and take on fearsome bosses. There are plenty to beat in 16 unique missions throughout the open world and each boss character drops unique loot and items.

GEAR AND ACCESSORIES

As you progress through the game, you'll be able to upgrade your gear and gather more powerful items. There are also lots of rare accessories to be found throughout the open world, but they'll take some finding!

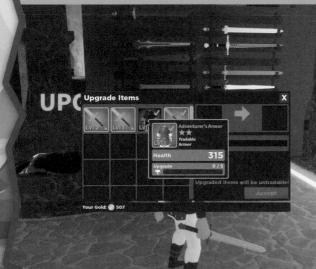

Upgrade Items

Adventurer's Armor
Tradable
Armor

Health   315
Upgrade   0 / 5

Upgraded items will be untradable!

Accept

Your Gold: 507

AWARD WINNER

World//Zero has been a massive hit with Roblox gamers and over 10 million players have checked it out to date. It even managed to pick up the 2020 Bloxy Award for Best Use of Tech, which is a huge result!

Creator: BRIBBLECO™
Release Date: May 2017
Genre: Adventure

CLEANING SIMULATOR

Don't you just hate it when your room gets all mucky? If your house looks like an actual rubbish tip, then learn how to tidy it up with this crazy simulation game that will have you cleaning like crazy!

HARD AT WORK

In Cleaning Simulator, you get to play as one of up to 40 janitors applying for a job to work at BRIBBLECO™. Clean up any mess you can find and keep things looking nice and shiny to progress through the game.

Grab me to talk to me!

MODEL EMPLOYEE

When you begin the game, you'll meet this strange orange fella. This is Scrombobulous Dringlebrapton, or CS for short and he gives you some handy tips and instructions to get started in your new career.

TOOLS OF THE TRADE

Before you begin your job, you'll need to grab the correct supplies. Grab a mop for cleaning up puddles and spray for getting rid of any yucky stains. If you run out of water, just dunk it in water for a refill.

SPARKLING AND SHINING

Some of those dirty marks and stubborn spots will take a lot of elbow grease to get fully clean. Keep using the mop and spray until sparkly stars appear and then you'll know the muck has all gone.

	Rarity	Won Yesterday	
	2.6% (Insane)	326	155731
Clean Boy Fully clean the BRIBBLECO™ grounds with the Tougher Job mode disabled. (Unlocks Owen the Onion)			
CLEAN BOY	Rarity 1.3% (Insane)	Won Yesterday 166	Won Ever 172308
Best Janitor Around Fully clean the BRIBBLECO™ grounds with the Tougher Job mode enabled. (Unlocks Paul the Potato)			
BEST JANITOR AROUND	Rarity 0.3% (Impossible)	Won Yesterday 36	Won Ever 59615
The Hidden Treasure Where could it be? (Unlocks Chris the Cherry)			
THE HIDDEN TREASURE	Rarity 9.4% (Extreme)	Won Yesterday 1164	Won Ever 601325
A Lemon Without Omelettes This one may be tough to get... (Unlocks Lucas the Lemon)			
A LEMON W/O OMELETTES	Rarity 4.4% (Insane)	Won Yesterday 552	Won Ever 320626

CLEANING CHARACTERS

There are all sorts of characters for players to choose from in the game and it's possible to unlock more by completing tasks or entering codes. You can also buy more characters and items from the Catalog.

FLING A THING

One very quick way of tidying up an office is to chuck things out of the window! You'll need to break the glass first before throwing items outside though and it will still be there when you exit the building.

TIDY UP TOYS

With over 24 million visits to date, the game has been a massive hit. What's more, you can actually buy real Cleaning Simulator toys that include special codes to download all sorts of unique in-game items!

SUPER BOMB SURVIVAL

Creator: Polyhex
Release Date: June 2014
Genre: Survival

Look, up in the sky... it's raining bombs! Try your luck at this awesome physics-based survival game and see how long you and your friends can last. One wrong step and you might just be blown to pieces!

OFF WITH A BANG

The main aim of this game is to see if you can survive for two and a half minutes while tons of explosives drop from above or pop up from below. Players start off by voting for three maps before the game begins.

BOMBS, BOMBS, BOMBS!

There are all kinds of crazy bombs to avoid and each type has a different affect. There are standard bombs, Soccerbombs, Zombombs, Shock Mines, Air Strikes, Cluster Rockets, Nukes, Homing Missiles and more!

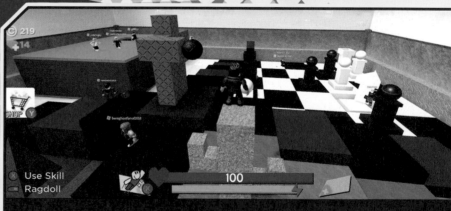

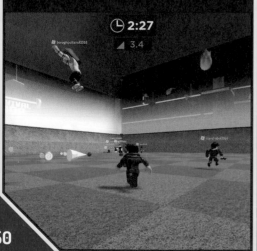

DUCK AND DODGE

When a new round begins, lots of different bombs will start dropping from the sky. Some of these are more lethal than others and, as the game goes on, they get much bigger and even replaced by more powerful ones.

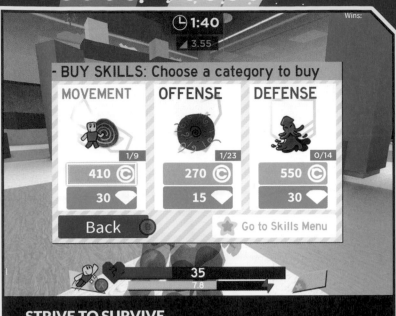

STRIVE TO SURVIVE

To last each round players will need to use various skills, boosts and tricks to avoid being blown up. It's possible to buy additional skills for the three available categories: Offence, Defence and Movement.

DROP 'N' GRAB

While playing through each level, items will be dropped that are worth grabbing. These include coins for buying more skills, gems, chicken drumsticks and heart capsule healing items and more.

SUPER SKILLS

At the start of a round, players can choose from a number of skills to help them survive. You could go for the Super Jump, Forcefield, Stun Pulse or others, but only one skill can be activated at a time.

EPIC EVENTS

Sometimes during rounds, a special event will kick off for 35 seconds. These can range from all players being powered up or getting double coins, to no skills and giant pianos dropping from the sky!

Creator: Olympic Gymnast Competition
Release Date: December 2016
Genre: Sport

GYMNASTICS GYMNASIUM

Now you can get your Roblox avatar leaner and fitter with this great sports simulation! Take part in regular monthly online competitions and fun events to learn all kinds of new gymnastic skills and routines.

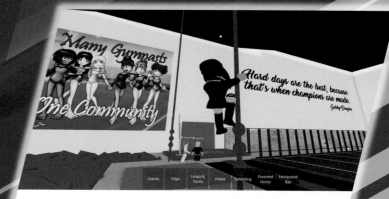

BEST OF THE BEST
The game is part of a competition group of online players who compete to show off their athletic abilities. You don't need to have any actual skills in real life, as the game is more about timing and rhythm.

SOMETHING FOR EVERYONE
Players can choose from a variety of fun sporting activities to try and improve their skills. These include balance beam, vault, floor, uneven bars, horizontal bar, pommel horse and many others.

GYMNASTIC RANKS
First time players will enter the game at the standard Gymnast rank, allowing them to compete and enter events. By taking part in competitions and winning, you could even become Gymnast of the Month!

HOW TO QUALIFY

To complete each activity, you'll have to correctly perform a series of moves on each section of the gym. Mastering forward flips, rotations, split leaps and other moves is essential to progress in the competition.

WARM UP

Just as in real life, it's best to do a few warm up activities before moving on to the main events. These could be something as simple as laps around the mat, stretching, runs and basic flips.

MONTHLY COMPETITIONS

There's a new online competition set every month, allowing players to try out their skills against other athletes. The bronze, silver and gold winners in each category have their names shown in a YouTube video!

TEAM TOYS

As with other Roblox games, there are even collectible Gymnastics Gymnasium toys! Dylan and Olivia are part of the Series 5 Celebrity and Series 7 Action mystery boxes and include codes for in-game items.

SPEED RUN 4

Creator: Vurse
Release Date: October 2014
Genre: Adventure

If you think you're as fast as lightning and as quick as the wind, then here's the perfect Roblox game for you! Race against the clock over challenging maps to see if you're a champion racer.

THE NEED FOR SPEED

This epic speedrunning game allows players to race through a number of different maps against a timer. You can have a go at each level as many times as you like to try and beat your personal best score.

PRIZE WINNER

Every time you complete a speed run, you'll be rewarded with lots of glittering Rubies. These add up every time you finish a map, so it's possible to collect an infinite number of Rubies in the game.

ON YOUR MARKS

To take part in a race, start by selecting one of the 31 levels that are available. Cross the start line to be automatically placed in sprint mode and then you have to make it to the finish as fast as you can.

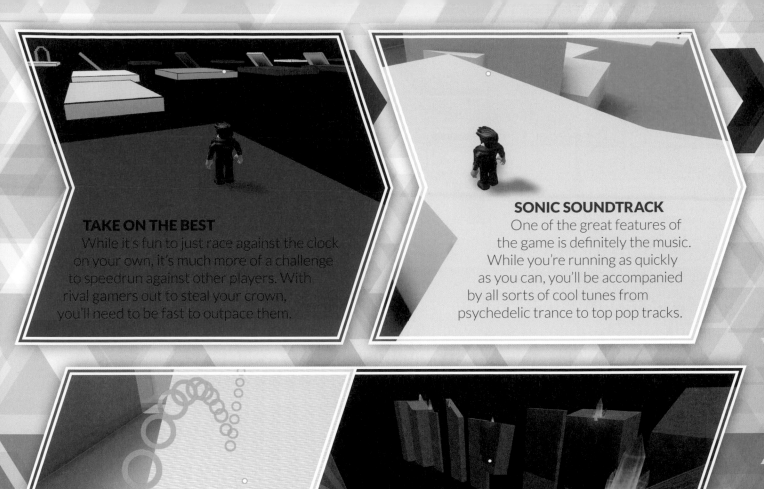

TAKE ON THE BEST
While it's fun to just race against the clock on your own, it's much more of a challenge to speedrun against other players. With rival gamers out to steal your crown, you'll need to be fast to outpace them.

SONIC SOUNDTRACK
One of the great features of the game is definitely the music. While you're running as quickly as you can, you'll be accompanied by all sorts of cool tunes from psychedelic trance to top pop tracks.

FAST-PACED EXTRAS
Developer Vurse is always adding great new features to the game, to keep players coming back time and again. These have included a mirror mode, multiple universes, zombie mode and much more.

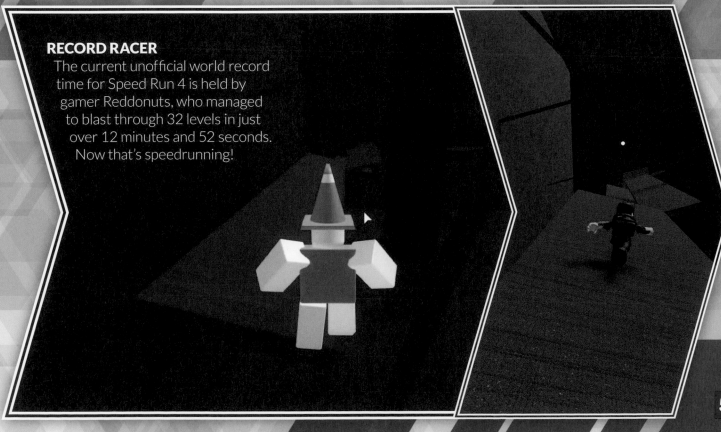

RECORD RACER
The current unofficial world record time for Speed Run 4 is held by gamer Reddonuts, who managed to blast through 32 levels in just over 12 minutes and 52 seconds. Now that's speedrunning!

CREATOR CHALLENGES

The team at Roblox is always coming up with new gameplay features and extras for players to try out. These include regular Creator Challenges, allowing gamers to try out their skills for special rewards.

BLOX BLOG

You can find out all about forthcoming and past challenges by heading over to the official Roblox Blog. This is the place to read about special events, what's required to complete them and the exclusive prizes.

SPECIAL THEMES

Sometimes the Creator Challenges are fairly straightforward game builds, but there are also often unique themed events to try. These have included such movies as *Star Wars*, *Godzilla: King of the Monsters* and *Jurassic World*!

CREATOR CHALLENGE
PRIZES

EXCLUSIVE PRIZES

If you take part in a Creator Challenge, you could win some very cool prizes. These can range from unique in-game items for your avatar to big cash prizes. Winners also get their games highlighted in the Catalog.

DESIGN YOUR OWN AVATAR

In May 2020, a blog post revealed how creators could enter the Avatar Design Contest. Imaginative players could send in images of their own bundle creations and see their finished designs for sale in the Avatar Shop.

AWARD WINNERS

Challenging and encouraging young creators to explore their imaginations in Roblox has led to some coders winning big awards. The 2017 National STEM Video Game Challenge was won by the Roblox game, Intervene!

SPEED BUILD

In November 2018 Roblox hosted the Build Your First Game in One House Challenge to encourage kids to start coding. Using free tools, young Robloxians could work against the clock to complete a quiz.

NOOBS VS PROS

The Roblox Tournaments are the place where players, developers and Roblox staff can go head-to-head in tough competitions. These are streamed live on the Roblox Twitch channel for all to watch.

SO YOU WANT TO MAKE YOUR OWN GAMES?

Once you've played a few Roblox games, you might be inspired to make your own. After all, almost every single game available on Roblox was created by players just like yourself!

Roblox provides all sorts of opportunities to learn how to design games. Once you've figured out how to do it, you can immediately release your creation to a community that's eager for more content.

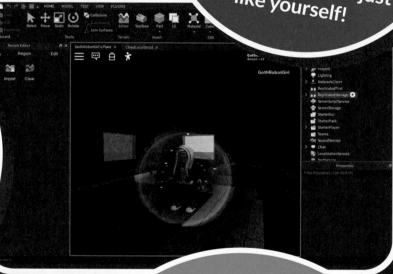

BRAINSTORM!
The first thing to do is to come up with a basic idea. It helps to write it down, or draw pictures to show what your game could look like. Answer the questions below to give you an idea of what kind of games you could try making:

What's your favourite game?

What genres do you like best? (Action, driving, obby?)

What game activities do you enjoy?

Do you like solo or multiplayer games?

What's your favourite theme? (Fantasy, RPG, sports, Sci-Fi?)

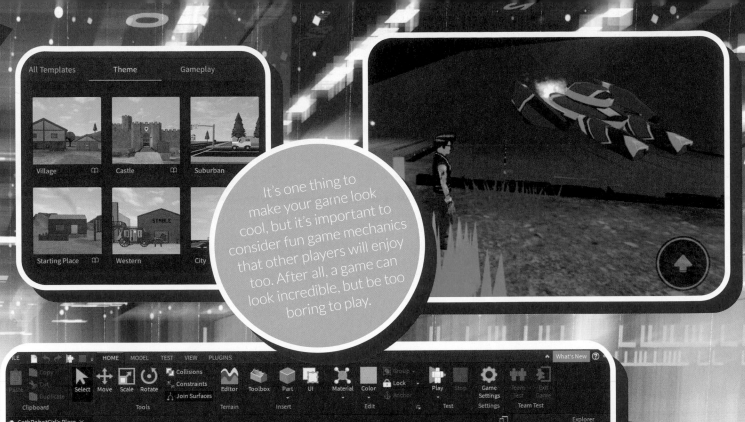

It's one thing to make your game look cool, but it's important to consider fun game mechanics that other players will enjoy too. After all, a game can look incredible, but be too boring to play.

SEE WHAT OTHERS HAVE DONE
Stumped about what kind of game to make? Just play some more! By trying some of the best games on the platform, you can see what people like and also what Roblox is capable of. See how people are interacting with those kinds of games and take notes.

GO SOCIAL

Roblox is a social game and you'll want to see how and why people choose the games they do. What kinds of mechanics keep players engaged? Talk to friends about what parts of a game they enjoy – it will help give you ideas for your own games!

GET STARTED

Roblox has a number of tutorials that show you how to make basic games.

You can choose from a number of genres that you might enjoy. Complete the tutorial and you'll have a simple framework to build on with anything you like!

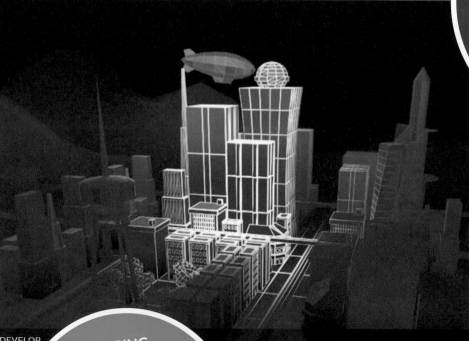

◆ Developer

Quick Start   Learn Roblox   API Re

RDC 2

Roblox Developer Conference 2019

Keynote presentations and insight fr...

DEVELOPMENT DISCUSSIONS

Precision Building

How to accomplish it and the benefits

DEVELOP

HELPING HANDS

Need more help getting started? Then head to www.developer.roblox.com for tutorials and a thriving developer community that can give you a hand!

R   Start

New   ide and reference.

DEVELOPER NEWS AND ANNOUNCEMENTS

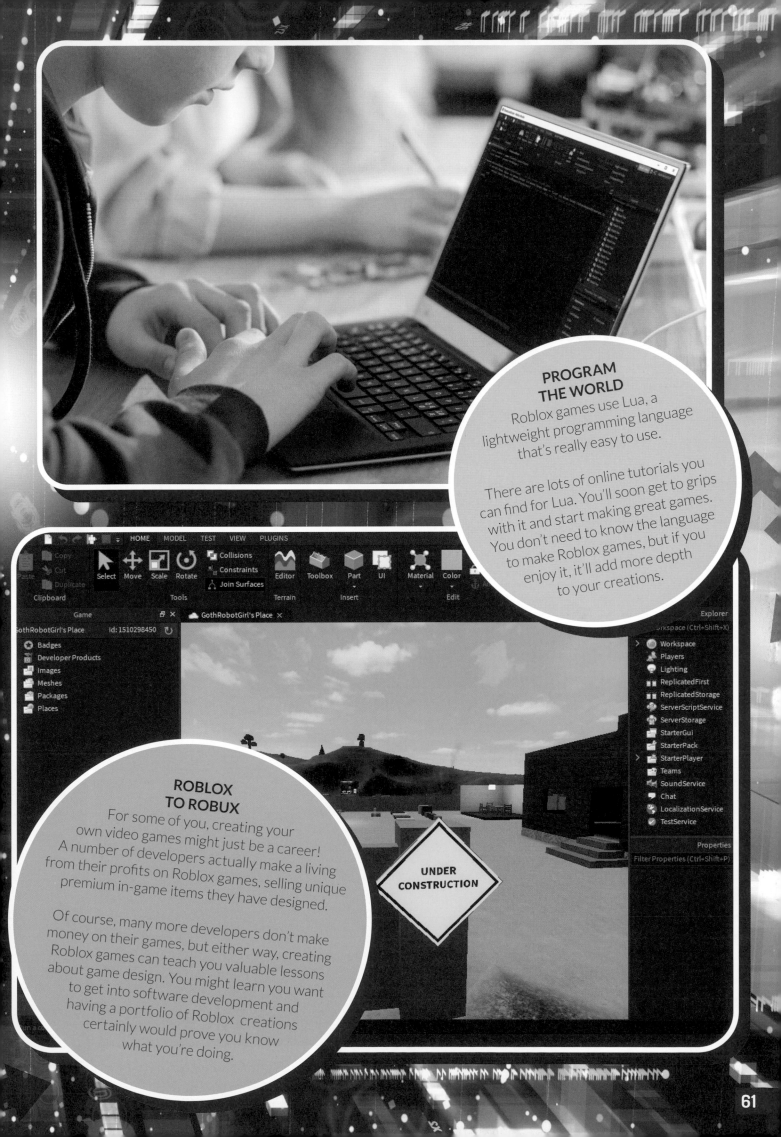

PROGRAM THE WORLD

Roblox games use Lua, a lightweight programming language that's really easy to use.

There are lots of online tutorials you can find for Lua. You'll soon get to grips with it and start making great games. You don't need to know the language to make Roblox games, but if you enjoy it, it'll add more depth to your creations.

ROBLOX TO ROBUX

For some of you, creating your own video games might just be a career! A number of developers actually make a living from their profits on Roblox games, selling unique premium in-game items they have designed.

Of course, many more developers don't make money on their games, but either way, creating Roblox games can teach you valuable lessons about game design. You might learn you want to get into software development and having a portfolio of Roblox creations certainly would prove you know what you're doing.

UNDER CONSTRUCTION

CREATING WITH ROBLOX STUDIO

This free tool lets you build your very own games! Roblox Studio is available for Windows and Mac, so just jump on your laptop or desktop and log in with your Roblox account.

DESIGN WHAT YOU KNOW
The tool allows you to make anything you can imagine. However, it can be overwhelming to look at all of these options when you first boot up the studio. Take it slow, play around with the sample game you're given and see how it all fits together. You'll learn by doing!

It might help to start off by building a place you're familiar with. Why not try to recreate your home or school? It's good practice and gives you an idea of how to design maps.

START LARGE

When you sit down to make your own game, you might be tempted to start working on all of the little details. However, we'd recommend getting the world situated first. Focus on the actual space of the map right from the start, building the terrain using tools such as grow, erode and smooth. No one wants to play on a single flat piece of land, so give it plenty of variety! You can add structures, mountains, lakes and even hidden tunnels snaking through the world. Just don't worry about the little stuff yet – that will come.

TEST, TEST AND TEST AGAIN

Every time you add something new to your game, you should test it. If you add something that breaks the game or makes it laggy, you'll immediately know what the problem is and how to tackle it. If you go a long time without testing your project and there's an issue, you'll need to make tons of changes to fix what went wrong! As you add things, you can get a better idea of what works and modify your plans accordingly.

63

MAKE SURE IT RUNS!

Have you ever started a Roblox game and been hit with lots of lag? If the game is choppy and chugs along at a terrible frame rate, it may be because the designer added too much stuff. You can optimise the game by making sure you don't overload the world with highly complex objects. Everyone wants to have a beautiful world, but sometimes you need to sacrifice detail for game speed and reliability.

GUI

The GUI (Graphical User Interface) is the information that's displayed to players that's not part of the game – things like their health, amount of cash and items. Designing a game with unique features means that you'll need a unique GUI. Make sure you don't go overboard and clutter the screen with dozens of pieces of information though. Also don't leave off important details anyone may need while playing your game!

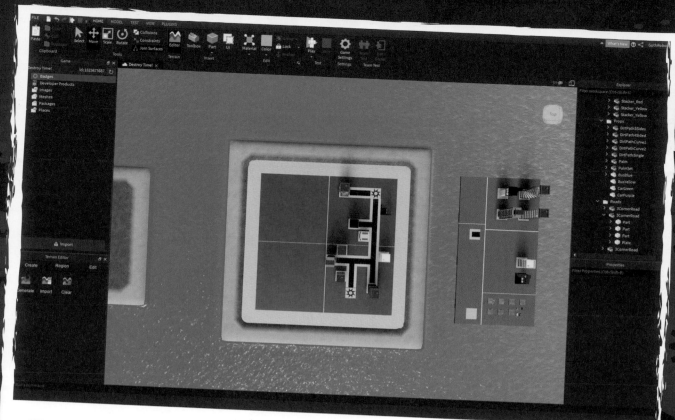

THE FUN FACTOR

This is what everyone strives for. Simply put, is the game fun to play? Do people enjoy themselves and want to keep playing? You're going to want to make sure there are plenty of exciting activities for your players, a satisfying loop that will keep people coming back. Test the game with multiple players and figure out how to encourage them to have things to do as a team.

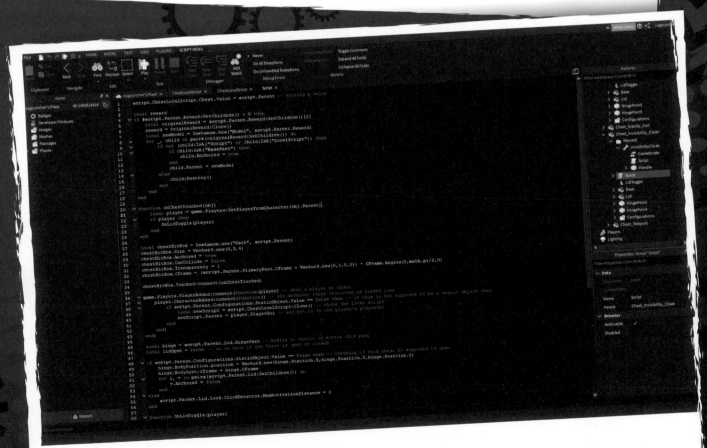

FOR ADVANCED USERS: SCRIPTING

To really make your creation different from the rest, you'll need to up your programming skills. Roblox uses the Lua language, so look online for resources and get learning. The use of scripts can make your game much more interactive and it will stand out from the pack.

ROBLOX EDUCATION

LEARNING REAL SKILLS WITH ROBLOX

Want to take your gaming skills to the next level? Then the Roblox Education programme can help you!

The Roblox Education programme offers students and teachers free online resources for almost every aspect of game design, including coding, game design, digital citizenship and entrepreneurial skills.

Thanks to this programme over 100 organisations worldwide, including schools and coding camps use Roblox for their classes. However, if your school isn't teaching Roblox or you can't make it to a coding camp, the good news is that there are six lesson plans available online that anyone can take advantage of.

While some classes use Minecraft in their lessons, you can only modify an existing game. In Roblox you make your very own creations using a real-world programming language, helping you learn coding.

Roblox uses Lua, a super-simple scripting language. It's not a drag and drop language, such as the one programs like Scratch and Tynker use. It's widely used for game development, so if you start to really enjoy making Roblox games, it's important to understand. Some say it's even easier to learn than Python programme, so it might be a good choice for your first programming language. Roblox offers lessons that will teach you the essentials, such as strings, arrays, and loops.

Creating New Scripts

Scripts are commonly created in **ServerScriptService**, a special folder for holding and running scripts.

1. In the Explorer, hover over **ServerScriptService** to see the ⊕ .

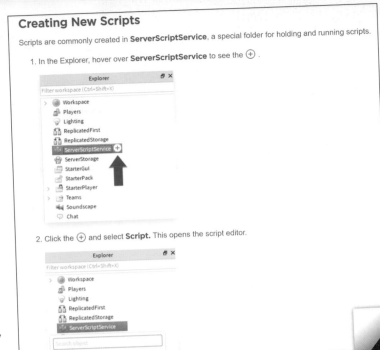

2. Click the ⊕ and select **Script.** This opens the script editor.

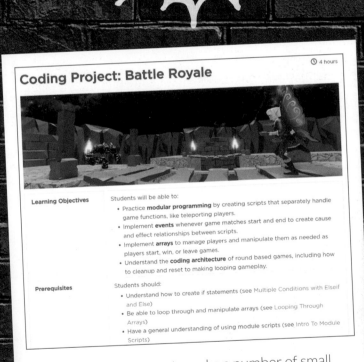

Education

Intro to Coding Cheatsheet

Create New Scripts	Run Code
Right-click object > Insert New Script	Press Play.

Print Function	Comments
Displays text on the screen. • Example: `print("Hello world!")`	Green notes saying what the code does. • Example: `--Turns PracticePart green`

Variables
Placeholders for information the program will use later. Variables can be changed and worked with in a variety of ways.

String Variables	Numerical Variables
Holds groups of letters and/or numbers. Uses quotation marks. Example: `"This is a string"` In use: `print("5 is my favorite")`	Used to count things Does not have quotation marks. Example: `5` In use: `wait(3)`

Properties
Any characteristic of an object.
Examples include color, visibility, speed, and health points.

Dot notation
Used to separate names of objects, properties, and keywords like "new".
Example: `game.Workspace.PartName.BrickColor = BrickColor.new(0, 0, 8, 0, 1)`

The Roblox Education programme may be intended for teachers, but anyone who wants to be a Roblox developer will find it handy. On the site you'll find free coding tips and tutorials, handy work sheets and even full game projects! Print out some of the cheat sheets they offer and keep them by your computer for easy access while you work on your lessons.

Coding Project: Battle Royale

⏱ 4 hours

Learning Objectives	Students will be able to:
	• Practice **modular programming** by creating scripts that separately handle game functions, like teleporting players.
	• Implement **events** whenever game matches start and end to create cause and effect relationships between scripts.
	• Implement **arrays** to manage players and manipulate them as needed as players start, win, or leave games.
	• Understand the **coding architecture** of round based games, including how to cleanup and reset to making looping gameplay.
Prerequisites	Students should:
	• Understand how to create if statements (see Multiple Conditions with Elseif and Else)
	• Be able to loop through and manipulate arrays (see Looping Through Arrays)
	• Have a general understanding of using module scripts (see Intro To Module Scripts)

The lessons allow you to make a number of small but completely functional games. Once you get the basics down, there are so many resources available to expand your creations and really make something special. You'll be having so much fun making the game (and having your friends play something you made) that you won't even realize that you're learning!

Players begin Roblox with a fairly basic look for their avatars, but it is possible to change, buy and create new skins. This allows you to have a customised character that will stand out from the crowd and impress your mates!

Avatar Editor

R6 R15

3D

Body Type   0%

Scaling options are available under Body category. Check **Body > Scale**

Got it

Packages have been moved to Costumes. Check **Costumes > Preset Costumes**

Got it

Avatar isn't loading correctly?

Redraw

Explor...

Recent ⌄   Clothing ⌄   Body ⌄

Recent > All

Man   Smile   Man Left Arm   Man Right Leg

Man Right   Man Left Leg   Man Torso   Man Head   Man
Arm

Brown Hair   Jean Shorts   Green Jersey   Black Jeans   ROB
              with White   with Sneakers   Tors

              ROBLOX Boy   ROBLOX Boy   ROBLOX Bo
              ft Leg   Right Arm   Left Arm

CUSTOMISE AVATARS

To change the look of your character, head on over to the Avatar Editor page and click on any of the pull down menus. You'll be able to add and remove items to wear, change skin colour and much more.

BUY SKINS

If you don't feel confident spending time creating your own skins, then you can always use Robux to purchase them. Skins can be bought from the Avatar Shop and other players and there are loads to choose from.

Featured Items on Roblox

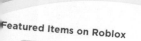

Horse Face & Fallon
◎ 400

Toy Animation Pack
◎ 250

Korblox Deathspeaker
◎ 17,000

Stitchface
◎ 4,000

Skeleton
◎ 500

Bear Face Mask
◎ 100

etro Sunglasses
Ayzria
80

Robot Animation Pack
◎ 80

Bubbly Animation
◎ 250

AVATAR SHOP

The Avatar Shop is absolutely packed with almost every character item you can imagine. From clothes and accessories, to character faces and animations. Some are free and others costs a lot of Robux.

FREE STUFF

There are always loads of free items you can grab from the Avatar Shop to customise your character. Select 'Categories' from the menu and then 'Price (Low to High)' to check out all the goodies!

MOBILE AVATAR EDITOR

If you have an iOS or Android mobile device, you can even edit your avatar on the go! Customise any element of your character that you like, then you can preview it before adding it to your game.

LICENSED AVATARS

Roblox has done crossovers with all sorts of licensed brands over the years, from Jurassic Park and Dr. Seuss to Star Wars and Doctor Who. Some of these options are only available for a short time, so get them while you can!

BBC
DOCTOR WHO
MARCH 12TH - 26TH, 2020
ROBLOX

ick Jeans with
Vhite Shoes
Free

ROBLOX Jacket
Free

eauti
leans
ree

coca cola
By danjo
Free

Roy-G-Biv
By kaze
Free

Money necklace #
By robosapien626
Free

Guitar Tee with
Black Jacket
ree

My Favorite Pizza
Shirt
Free

General pants
pilot wars
By robobliz
Free

THE CRAZIEST
ROBLOX EVENTS!

Roblox is constantly adding fun new events to keep people entertained! There are a number of these every year and they allow players to get limited-time exclusive items, just for playing along. These are some of the best and most recent ones...

RDC
RPC 19
roblox
developers
conference

ROBLOX DEVELOPERS CONFERENCE

Every year the best and brightest developers on the Roblox platform join together for a weekend of events and activities, all in the aim of brainstorming new experiences for players. A lot of it is broadcast live, allowing even non-developers to get in on the fun, watching all the presentations, game jams and tournaments.

STRANGER THINGS

To celebrate the third season of the hit Netflix show, Roblox offered riddles and puzzles for Robloxians to solve. They dropped clues over their social media channels that led to codes that would unlock limited-time items, such as a Scoops Ahoy Hat and a Demogorgon mask!

PIZZA PARTY

For this event, all players were given special Pizza Launcher items that allowed them to shoot pizzas everywhere! The developer offered all kinds of prizes for getting shot by a pizza in specific games. An obvious event for giant turtles trained in martial arts.

GALACTIC SPEEDWAY CREATOR CHALLENGE

There have been a few Star Wars events in Roblox, but the most recent one allowed you to make your very own driftspeeder and challenge other players. You were also able to earn amazing items from the Star Wars universe by completing coding and game design lessons. Awesome!

POWERS

A source of strange power appeared in the Roblox world, which lured mobs of zombies to come and get it. Robloxians teamed up with friends in order to fight off the hordes and forge legendary crystal swords to aid their battles! This event used the Swordburst 2, Zombie Rush and Pirate Simulator games for its events and included many cool prizes.

PRIZES

EGG HUNT 2019: SCRAMBLED IN TIME

This was the tenth annual Egg Hunt! A staggering 42 games took place in this one event, which was sponsored by Avengers: Endgame. There were a total of 58 eggs available to find and collecting the specific Avengers eggs would earn you the ultimate power of the Infinity Gauntlet.

GODZILLA CREATOR CHALLENGE

This giant-lizard themed challenge had players rushing to complete coding lessons in Roblox Studio and then take a quiz to see what they'd learned. If this sounds like homework, well, it was worth it. Completing the challenge by answering all the questions correctly earned players items such as Rodan's Head, a Godzilla Spine Backpack, and Ghidorah's Wings. You even got to try a game where you play as Godzilla and smash up a city!

WRESTLEMANIA

For this event WWE offered a deal unlike any other – free prizes with no games or tasks to complete! You didn't need to worry about learning how to wrestle, you just had to go to the Roblox catalog and grab these items, allowing you to earn your very own Championship belt without doing a thing!

This annual event celebrates the best of Roblox. Users can vote for their favourite creators, as well as earn limited items by playing specific games and taking part in a scavenger hunt. Categories includes Favourite Map, Best Video Channel, and Best Lobby.

RB BATTLES

Also known as 'Roblox Battles', this was a YouTube tournament. 16 famous creators competed in a number of different games in order to get the grand prize. The winner was KreekCraft, who received the one-of-a-kind Champion's Swordpack, and 1,000,000 Robux! Users were able to get in on the action by voting on who they thought would win the tournament, with those who guessed correctly winning the Shield of Wisdom.

DECORATE THE OFFICE

This unique event challenged Robloxians to create posters that would be put up in the Roblox offices! A lot of people took pictures of physical items they created, everything from go-karts to tree houses. Winners also received an exclusive Sunderfire Headdress to show off.

you can imagine it,

You can build it

ROBLOX DURING LOCKDOWN

One way to keep busy and have safe fun at home during 2020 was to play Roblox. As well as taking part in and creating games, players could also watch a special one-of-kind live world record-breaking concert event!

ONE WORLD: TOGETHER AT HOME

This incredible global digital broadcast took place on April 18th and featured some of the biggest musical acts and celebrities on the planet, all giving their time to raise awareness to help others during the COVID-10 pandemic.

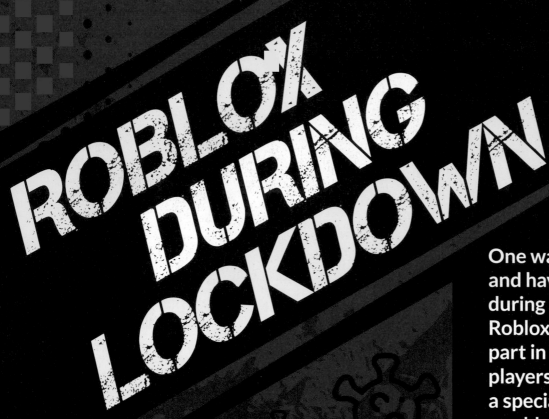

ONE WORLD
TOGETHER AT HOME

GLOBAL CITIZEN.

ROBLOX

CURATED IN COLLABORATION WITH LADY GAGA

STAR-STUDDED EVENT

Organised by Lady Gaga, the concert featured all sorts of huge names. There were songs from the likes of Chris Martin, Elton John and Jessie J, as well as appearances from David Beckham, Lewis Hamilton and LL Cool J!

APPEARANCES BY:

ADAM LAMBERT • ALICIA KEYS • AMY POEHLER • ANDRA DAY • ANDREA BOCELLI • ANGÈLE • ANITTA • ANNIE LENNOX • AWKWAFINA • BECKY G • BEN PLATT • BILLIE EILISH • BILLIE JOE ARMSTRONG • BILLY RAY CYRUS • BLACK COFFEE • BRIDGET MOYNAHAN • BURNA BOY • CAMILA CABEL • • CASSPER NYOVEST • CELINE DION • CHARLIE PUTH • CHRIS MARTIN • CHRISTINE AND THE QUEENS • COMMON • CONNIE BRITTON • DANAI GURIRA • DAVID & VICTORIA BECKHAM • DELTA GOODREM • DON CHEADLE • EASON CHAN • EDDIE VEDDER • ELLEN DEGENERES • ELLIE GOULDIN • • ELTON JOHN • ERIN RICHARDS • FINNEAS • HEIDI KLUM • HOZIER • HUSSAIN AL JASMI • IDRIS AND SABRINA ELBA • J BALVIN • JACK BLACK • JACK JOHNSON • JACKY CHEUNG • JAMEELA JAMIL • JAMES MCAVOY • JASON SEGEL • JENNIFER HUDSON • JENNIFER LOPEZ • JESS GLYNNE • JESSIE J • JESSIE REYEZ • JIMMY FALLON • JIMMY KIMMEL • JOHN LEGEND • JUANES • KACEY MUSGRAVES • KEITH URBAN • KERRY WASHINGTO • KESHA • LADY ANTEBELLUM • LADY GAGA • LANG LANG • LESLIE ODOM JR. • LEWIS HAMILTON • LIAM PAYNE • LILI REINHART • LILLY SINGH • LILY TOMLIN • LINDSEY VONN • LISA MISHRA • LIZZO • LL COOL J • LOLA LENNOX • LUIS FONSI • LUPITA NYONG'O • MALUMA • MAREN MORRIS • MATT BOMER • MATTHEW MCCONAUGHEY • MEGAN RAPINOE • MICHAEL BUBLÉ • MILKY CHANCE • NAOMI OSAKA • NATTI NATASHA • NIALL HORAN • NOMZAMO MBATHA • OPRAH WINFREY • PAUL MCCARTNEY • PHARRELL WILLIAMS • P.K. SUBBAN • PICTURE THIS • PRIYANKA CHOPR • JONAS • RITA ORA • SAM HEUGHAN • SAM SMITH • SAMUEL L JACKSON • SARAH JESSICA PARKER • SEBASTIÁN YATRA • SHAH RUKH KHAN • SHAWN MENDES • SHERYL CROW • SHO MADJOZI • SOFI TUKKER • STEPHEN COLBERT • STEVIE WONDER • SUPERM • TAYLOR SWIFT • THE KILLERS • TIM GUNN • USHER • VISHAL MISHRA • ZUCCHERO

VIRTUAL THEATRE

To watch the event, players needed to head over to the game's virtual theatre at the correct time and see it broadcast live on the big screen. This venue was also used for the 7th Annual Bloxys awards.

SHOW YOUR SUPPORT

One way for Roblox players to show their support for the event was by wearing exclusive in-game items. These cool extras were free and included Solidarity Shades, Historic Headphones, Bravery Backpack and more.

SPECIAL QUESTS

As well as the exclusive in-game items, there were also special event mini quests that players could take part in before the concert. By collecting coins, it was possible to spend them on even more unique items.

RECORD BREAKER

One World: Together At Home was a huge success and a record-breaking event. According to Guinness World Records, the concert featured the most musical acts at a remote music festival and raised over £100 million!

TIPS AND TRICKS

FINDING GAMES

There are so many Roblox games that it can be hard finding anything really good to play! If you've already tried the games we've recommended in this book, you'll have to sift through thousands of others. So how do you find the real gems? Here's where the Roblox community comes in handy. Sort the games by 'Top Rated' and you'll see the ones people love best. Chances are if a lot of people like a particular game, it will be worth checking out!

Roblox uses the microphone to find players around you. We may increase your audio volume. Learn more.

Start Friending

⭐ Favorited	🔊 Follow	👍 1M+	👎 155K+

PLAY FAVOURITES

Make sure to mark games you enjoy with a star. This will add it to your favourites list, making it really easy to jump right back in! This will save you the trouble of sifting through countless clones to find the real game, too. Adding a thumbs up to the game will allow other players to see that it's great!

BRING YOUR FRIENDS ALONG

Roblox is a lot more fun as a community, so add your real-life friends to your list. You'll be able to see what they're playing and jump right into games with them. What's more, you'll be able to chat with them at any time, no matter what they're playing. You can even find their creations and play their own games!

Roblox

Roblox Corporation   Adventure
Action & Adventure

🎮 Everyone 10+   👑 Family Friendly

Offers in-app purchases

➕ Add to Wishlist

GET FREE ROBUX!!!

Hint – there's no such thing as free Robux. It's never, ever going to happen. Don't listen to anyone who tells you otherwise, they're likely scammers.

DOWNLOAD ALL THE ROBLOX

It might be nice to unwind with the Xbox One version of Roblox, but you might as well have it on your phone too, for quick games on the go! All your progress will stay the same, no matter which platform you play the game.

SHOWCASE

Try searching for 'Showcase' games. They're usually not much in the way of actual games, since they're pushing the platform to its limit, but they offer really beautiful experiences! You'll be amazed at the kind of stunning locations some developers were able to create with Roblox Studio.

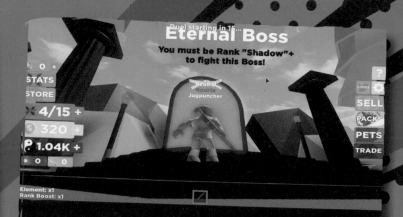

SHOW OFF YOUR SKILLS

Playing on Xbox One and just did something amazing in your game? Will your friends believe you when you tell them? Hit the Xbox button on your controller and then the X button to capture a screenshot, or Y to record a video of the last 30 seconds of gameplay.

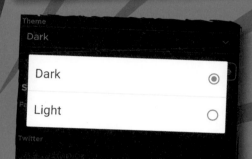

DARK MODE

Roblox on mobile has a dark theme for those who hate staring at bright white screens! Head to settings and Account Info. You'll see a drop-down menu called 'Theme'. Just tap it and select 'Dark', and enjoy your newfound darkness!

DON'T BE MEAN

It's a simple idea, but don't be mean to people on Roblox. Treat other players they way you'd want to be treated. Otherwise you run the risk of ruining someone's Roblox experience, or even getting reported and banned from the game if you keep it up!

FOLLOW ROBLOX

Keep up on Roblox's social media channels to stay on top of the latest events. They're constantly throwing special limited-time events that allow players to earn items that will soon disappear, so if you want to get in on the fun you have to stay in the know!

CREATOR CODES

There's no such thing as free Robux, but creators do have the ability to give away free in-game items. A lot of developers offer hidden codes that unlock things in their games. Hint – make sure to click on a developer's profile pages. A lot of them hide codes in their description, just for eagle-eyed players.

SEE SOMETHING YOU WANT? GRAB IT!

Roblox is famous for its limited-time events that offer up exclusive items. There are dozens of famous items that people wear that are no longer available. Make sure you get them before they're gone forever. Sure, you can always trade someone for an out-of-print item, but you'll pay for it. Some ultra-rare items like the Red Grind cap have sold for over 200,000 Robux!

STAYING SAFE, BEING SOCIAL

FOR PLAYERS

PICKING A USERNAME
NEVER choose a username that has your personal information, such as your real name or birthday.

STAY SECRET
Don't ever give out your real name, address, phone number, or the school you go to. Roblox will never need this info, and neither will anyone else. Roblox has chat software that will automatically try to filter out real-life names for a reason.

STAY IN-GAME
Scammers may ask you to trade money or items outside of the game. That's a good way to lose things. The trading menu in Roblox is designed to protect you, so stick to that and never give anything to people outside the game, no matter how trustworthy they may appear.

DON'T BE AFRAID TO REPORT
Players can easily mute and report inappropriate or abusive chat message, or disturbing content. Just use the Report Abuse system that's located on every single menu and Roblox will be notified and take action as soon as possible.

TELL YOUR PARENTS
Be brave. If someone is bothering you or you saw something you didn't like, tell a parent or guardian. Don't be afraid to say if someone is being inappropriate on Roblox. This game is for everyone and no one should be made to feel unsafe!

"I HEARD ABOUT A ROBUX GENERATOR!"
There are no such thing as Robux Generators – they're made up by scammers to steal money and accounts from players. Don't fall for it. Never trust any websites that aren't official. All official websites end with '.roblox.com'.

FOR PARENTS

BE INVOLVED
The best thing parents can do to make sure their children stay safe playing Roblox is to simply talk to them about the dangers. Make an account for yourself as you make one for your child. You'll even be able to add them as your child on Roblox, allowing you to ensure the social aspects of the game aren't getting in the way of them having fun.

SAFETY FEATURES
You can sign into your child's account and choose the level of privacy that they have. Make sure you choose the correct date of birth for your child as it sets the default security settings depending on how old they are. You can further modify the settings so that no one can contact your child, or that everyone can. Older players have more options.

MESSAGES AND CHAT
You can easily view your child's private message and chat histories from the main screen. You can also see your child's online friends, the games they've made, and anything they've purchased. If anything looks off, you can then take action.

PROTECTING YOUNGER CHILDREN
While Roblox is tamer than most games, some games feature violence or scary situations. You can go to the Account Restrictions section of your child's account to restrict them from playing anything too intense for their age group.

"MY KID IS BEING BULLIED"
If someone is bothering your child, you should report and block them. By clicking on a username you can easily block a user and prevent them from ever contacting your child. By reporting abuse you can make sure that Roblox is aware of the situation.

For many more resources we recommend going to Roblox's official parent's guide at: www.corp.roblox.com/parents
There you'll find tutorials for navigating the platform, as well as tips for online safety.